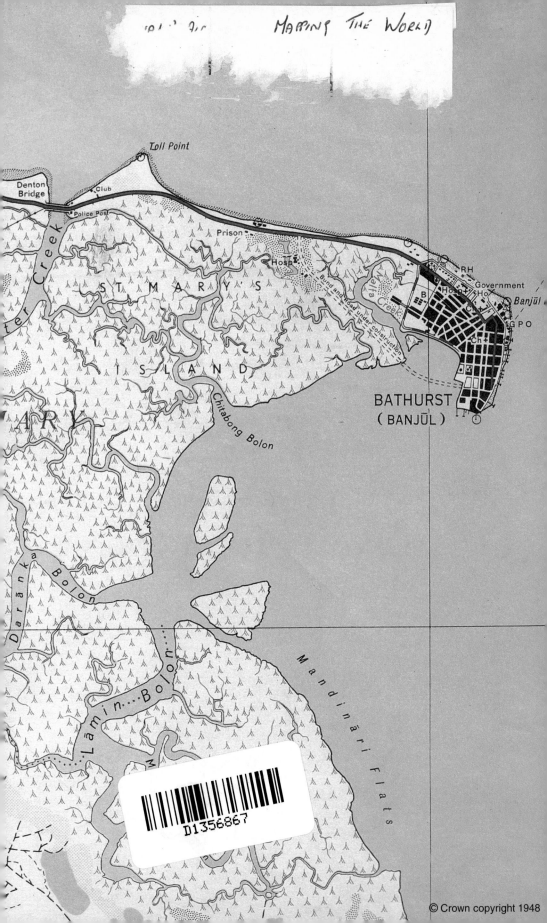

Toll Point

Denton
Bridge

Club

Police Post

ter Creek

Prison

Hosp.

ST MARY'S

ISLAND

Bund and road under construction

Malta Creek

RH

Government

Banjūl

Hosp

Ho

B

GPO

Ch

ARY

Chitabong Bolon

BATHURST
(BANJŪL)

Darānka Bolon

Lāmin Bolon

M

Mandināri Flats

MAPPING THE WORLD

Brigadier Martin Hotine, CMG CBE
Director 1946–1965
Painting (1963) by L D Carmichael, Chief Cartographer. Crown copyright

Ordnance Survey

Mapping the World

A History of the Directorate of Overseas Surveys 1946–1985

Alastair Macdonald

London: HMSO

© Crown Copyright 1996

Applications for reproduction should be made to HMSO Copyright Unit,
St Crispins, Duke Street, Norwich NR3 1PD

ISBN 0 11 701590 3

British Library Cataloguing in Publication Data
A CIP catalogue record for this book
is available from the British Library

Designed and edited by HMSO

Published by HMSO and available from:

HMSO Publications Centre
(Mail, fax and telephone orders only)
PO Box 276, London SW8 5DT
Telephone orders 0171 873 9090
General Enquiries 0171 873 0011
(queueing system in operation for both numbers)
Fax orders 0171 873 8200

HMSO Bookshops
49 High Holborn, London WC1V 6HB
(counter service only)
0171 873 0011 Fax 0171 831 1326
68–69 Bull Street, Birmingham B4 6AD
0121 236 9696 Fax 0121 236 9699
33 Wine Street, Bristol BS1 2BQ
0117 926 4306 Fax 0117 929 4515
9–21 Princess Street, Manchester M60 8AS
0161 834 7201 Fax 0161 833 0634
16 Arthur Street, Belfast BT1 4GD
01232 238451 Fax 01232 235401
71 Lothian Road, Edinburgh EH3 9AZ
0131 228 4181 Fax 0131 229 2734
The HMSO Oriel Bookshop
The Friary, Cardiff CF1 4AA
01222 395548 Fax 01222 384347

HMSO's Accredited Agents
(see Yellow Pages)

and through good booksellers

This book is dedicated to the men and women of all races who worked for the Directorate at home and overseas with such commitment, enthusiasm and humour.

Contents

List of Map Extracts

between pp 128 and 129

Map extracts on endpapers: front – Bathurst, The Gambia, Series DCS 15 Gambia 1:50,000 Sheet 10 First edition, 1948; back – Banjul (formerly Bathurst), Gambia (formerly The Gambia), DOS 415 Gambia 1:50,000 Sheet 10 Edition 5-Dos, 1981.
Crown copyright.

Foreword

by
Baroness Chalker of Wallasey,
Minister for Overseas Development

This is a story of unconventional men doing unconventional things in areas far from Britain's shores. That these men were Civil Servants and that their success materially aided the development of an area twice the size of Western Europe makes the story all the more memorable.

Alastair Macdonald has written the most difficult of all books – one which embodies both an official history and the human story. His sources have ranged from official files through published and unpublished articles to the diaries and reminiscences of Directorate of Overseas Surveys' (DOS) staff. No equivalent account could have been written in a few years time: many of the survivors of the early years are now octogenarians. He succeeds admirably through concentrating on a number of themes after an initial account of the founding of the DOS. Who would have thought (or known) that, in the darkest days of 1941, officials in Whitehall were planning the peace and including the need for mapping of the then Colonies to foster their development? The sense of Imperial responsibility for these far-flung areas of the world is highly evident in the pages of this book. Less glorious is the bitter acrimony revealed between Ordnance Survey and other parts of the War Office, only four days before war broke out in 1939, over who should have responsibility for the proposed survey and mapping overseas.

The Directorate existed for thirty-eight years. It was born in 1946, largely as the brainchild of one brilliant individual, Brigadier Martin Hotine, and succeeded through a combination of genius, effort and brigandry. Serendipity also played its full part: the fortuitous availability of Polish military staff who could not return to their country in 1946 provided a core of astonishingly independent and committed surveyors and cartographers. The exploits of DOS surveyors, culled from their experiences in some fifty-five countries of the world, read like a story of British heroes from John Buchan.

Those working at home, with RAF photography covering half a million square miles and with sometimes imperfect survey results, performed miracles of innovation to produce the early maps. In later years, with increasingly sophisticated equipment, they went on to produce quality products that received wide acclaim and won several prizes. Women were always well represented amongst the cartographers but, sadly, played no direct role in field work for many years though the chapter on the role of wives is immensely moving. It illustrates graphically the hardships suffered by those who joined their husbands and the fortitude expected of them. One other fascinating revelation is the vital contribution made by the indigenous employees of DOS in each of the countries surveyed which, in many cases, led to a long-standing comradeship between them and the British.

DOS was a creature of its time. In the best sense, its rationale and funding reflected a sense of duty and a determination on the part of British citizens and of British governments of the day to help other countries. There is still a real need for mapping and other geographical information. Topographic mapping forms the framework on which all other information is assembled; without it, all development, from the most elementary formulation of policy to the planning of operations, is liable to disaster. Today, half of the world is still unmapped at 1:50,000 scale and much of what exists is long out of date. In sharp contrast, Britain is mapped in a hundred times greater detail on average and this mapping underpins many of the activities of government, commerce and industry. But mapping now involves the use of satellite technology and computers rather than lengthy safaris; the information required is delivered as computer files rather than paper maps. And the provision of a detailed topographic framework is now much more a matter for the countries themselves.

The last years of the Directorate of Overseas Surveys were funded by the Overseas Development Administration (ODA). After 1984, it was merged with the Ordnance Survey (OS). ODA still funds some of the overseas activities undertaken by OS and its Director General remains the adviser on survey and mapping to my Department. When activities of any kind are discontinued, those committed to the enterprise understandably feel pain. But I hope that ODA's joint sponsorship of this book with OS demonstrates our high regard for those who, both in Britain and in many other countries, mapped large and inhospitable areas of the world for the Crown. Their contribution was magnificent and theirs is a story that should be told. We should be grateful to Alastair Macdonald for telling it, and telling it so well.

Chalker of Wallasey

Acknowledgements

It would have been impossible to have written this book on my own. I have relied to an enormous extent on the kindness of the many former employees of the Directorate who took the time and trouble to record some of their memories for my use. Inevitably, I received far more material than I could use and, sadly, I have had to leave out some excellent contributions. Those that I have included are acknowledged in the References.

The fact that the book was written at all is due to the enthusiasm and ingenuity of David Rhind, the Director General of the Ordnance Survey, who arranged the financing of the project. I am grateful to the Overseas Development Administration who also contributed to the costs of the project and to Ordnance Survey International who provided facilities for me during my research.

Edwin Furmston and Ian O'Brien provided much advice and encouragement. Richard Porter was the source of many useful ideas and helped a great deal with the location of old records. Much of Chapter 20 is based on a text that he supplied to me and he prepared Appendices 1, 2 and 3. Edwin, Ian and Richard all helped to improve my original draft.

My researches created extra work for Norrie Smith in the Ordnance Survey Registry. He arranged for the delivery and return of the large quantity of files that I required from the Public Records Office with quiet efficiency and good humour.

Finally, I would like to express my gratitude towards Richard Worsley, the copy-editor, for his meticulous scrutiny of my original typescript, for the clarity of his comments and for the logical approach he brought to the variable quality of my written English.

Author's Note

Almost all the British Colonies changed their names at Independence. I have adopted the convention of using the name which was current at the time of the events being related. Thus, an account of early days in primary triangulation might refer to Bechuanaland whilst the later experiences of married families in the bush in that country would refer to it as Botswana. A list of countries, showing both their pre- and their post-independence names, is supplied at Appendix 4.

The quotations in the book come from three main sources: Government files, Government Command Papers and private communications from former employees. The references to all three need some explanation.

I was able to inspect files held at the Public Record Office (PRO), some Directorate files still held by the Overseas Development Administration (ODA) and files still held by the Ordnance Survey (though some of the latter were destroyed under the approved procedures shortly after I had used them).

References to PRO files commence with 'PRO', and are followed by the class and item number (e.g., OD 5/178). The original file reference of the depositing department follows in brackets.

DOS files held by ODA are shown as 'ODA(DOS) File . . .' while OS files are shown as either 'OS(DOS) File . . .' or simply 'OS File . . .', depending on whether the file is part of the DOS archive transferred to OS but not incorporated into its system, or part of the official OS filing system.

Some individuals still possess copies of official correspondence where the DOS parent file has been destroyed. I have referenced extracts from these by the author of the letter and the phrase 'letter to . . .'.

There are a number of references to Government Command Papers. These have prefixes related to the year of publication as follows:

[1–4222]	1833–69
C1–9550	1870–99
Cd 1–9239	1900–1918
Cmd 1–9889	1919–56
Cmnd 1–9927	1956–86
Cm 1–	1986–

Note: the First Series has no letters prefix and the numbers here are given within square brackets.

There are a great number of personal reminiscences quoted in the book which have been extracted from communications sent to me by former members of staff: mostly from letters but, in a few cases, from substantial memoirs compiled but not published by individuals. Another useful source has been the archive of the Monthly Diaries submitted by field surveyors to Headquarters. Reminiscences from letters are referenced by a name and the phrase 'Personal Communication'. It is intended that the manuscript letters from which the quotations have been extracted will be brought together and deposited in the Ordnance Survey Library. References to memoirs use the name and the term 'Personal Memoir'. My own recollections, which have not been written down elsewhere, use my name and the term 'Personal Recollection'. Finally, extracts from Monthly Diaries are identified as such. At the time of writing, these were still held at the Ordnance Survey pending a decision on their future. All personal recollections, memoirs and letters are the property of the individuals concerned.

Introduction

On a cold afternoon in March 1955, an officer of the Royal Engineers, Captain Doug Arnott, and I entered an austere office in an undistinguished building alongside the railway track at Tolworth, Surrey. Behind an oak desk sat a man with hawk-like features and a shock of white hair. Behind him, covering one entire wall, was a vast map of Africa from Gambia in the west to Somaliland in the east and from the Sudan in the north to Basutoland in the south. Scattered across the surface of the map were a number of tiny white flags, each with a name, representing the locations of the surveyors under his command. After we had introduced ourselves as the newly trained recruits from No. 13 Long Survey Course, he sprang out of his chair and strode across to the map.

'Macdonald' he said, pointing slightly below and to the left of Kilimanjaro, 'you will be joining our survey party somewhere about here. You will be helping to run a chain of triangulation down here' – a sweeping motion down to his right as far as the Indian Ocean – 'and then' – another sweeping motion up the coast – 'up towards Mombasa and Malindi. You, Arnott, are going to Tanganyika. The survey party is based here.' – stooping slightly and pointing to a town with the mellifluous name of Morogoro – 'Your job is to run another chain of triangulation' – bending further still – 'down to Nachingwea in the south, to connect with the chain we have just completed' – a final swing to his left – 'across from Mbeya.'

The man whose sweeping arms were shaping our destinies was Lieutenant Colonel G J Humphries, known to all as Hum, who rejoiced in the impressive title of Deputy Director of Colonial Surveys. As he was finishing his description of our assignments, someone called him away from the office and we were left standing there, bubbling with excitement at what lay before us. I couldn't resist rushing up to the wall map and mimicking his arm movements as he moved us like pawns across the continent. Unfortunately, as my hyperactive arm reached the northern limit of the map, it dislodged the top map sheet and a whole line of them fell away from the board on which they were mounted, the drawing pins scattering over the floor. With Doug standing *cave* at the door, I frantically restored them to their place and, when Hum returned, we were standing politely in place by his desk waiting to hear the rest of his instructions.

So began my association with the Directorate of Colonial (Geodetic and Topographical) Surveys, an association which was to last for eighteen years all told. I had joined a department of the Home Civil Service which was about as far removed from the stereotype as it was possible to be. It was unconventional and exciting and it generated a level of commitment and a feeling of camaraderie that was sustained for the great majority of its employees throughout the years of its existence and beyond.

The Directorate was a unit set up by the Colonial Office in 1946, after two decades of lobbying by prominent scientists and land surveyors, who were concerned that Britain was not fulfilling its Imperial role of mapping its Colonial territories in the well-thought out manner of the Ordnance Survey at home. Its job was, first, to provide national geodetic frameworks throughout the Colonial Empire which would both contribute to man's understanding of the size and shape of the earth and provide the basis of accurate mapping and, secondly, to produce such mapping, using modern methods based on aerial photography. As the wind of change swept most of the Colonies to independence, the Directorate's remit was expanded to cover independent countries both within and without the Commonwealth. Its name was changed to the Directorate of Overseas Surveys in 1957 and it continued to undertake a wide range of geodetic and mapping tasks for a further twenty-eight years.

The work involved in these tasks was unusual, to say the least. In the field, it meant climbing mountains and camping on top, often for weeks on end, walking long distances through dry, featureless plains and damp rain forest or crossing the surf surrounding a Pacific island in a boat that seemed too flimsy for the job. At home, the enormous amount of mapping to be done called for innovation and improvisation, constantly searching at the leading edge of technology for new techniques that would significantly increase the rate of production. The unusual nature of the work naturally enough attracted some unusual characters, especially in the field, and controlling them from a distance of several thousand miles became something of an art for the Directors involved.

The fact that the Directorate was set up in the first place, and the character of the organisation that emerged, was very much due to the personality and the efforts of one man, its first Director, Brigadier Martin Hotine CMG CBE. Hotine was a man of exceptional talent, great personal charm and rumbustious temperament. He was described in an obituary as the most accomplished mathematician never to be made a Fellow of the Royal Society. There could be two reasons for this omission: he was a self-taught mathematician, having abandoned a Cambridge degree course in his youth, and he always said exactly what he felt, often in rather colourful metaphors. However, though he could often savage a colleague in an argument, he could also spend the rest of the day fighting to get that same colleague a fair deal over his pension rights.

Certainly, the excitement that I felt on that first day in Humphries' office never left me and I hope that, in the pages that follow, I will be able to communicate to the reader the excitement, the fun, the sense of achievement and the comradeship that were the essential ingredients of this unique organisation.

Unique it may have been; perfect it certainly was not. Over the years, there were, of course, criticisms of the Directorate from Whitehall administrators, from overseas Survey Departments and from individual employees. Like any organisation, it made its mistakes but this book does not set out to identify and analyse them. It is not that sort of book – nor is it an academic evaluation of its mapping processes and production. This has already been made by Professor Gerald McGrath, who also worked for the Directorate as a young field surveyor. [1] My book is intended to be a social history; it might be more accurate to call it just a story of some of the people who were caught up in its achievements. The scope of the Directorate's activities is so large, spread over so many countries and so many years, that a full history would be a mammoth task. I have therefore had to make choices – personal choices – over what to include and what to leave out. These choices have been influenced to some extent by my own memory of the Directorate as I experienced it but, to a much greater extent, by the sources that have been available to me.

The Directorate does not always appear to have clearly separated policy from operational matters in its filing systems and one result is that its relationship with its parent department is not always easy to follow. The files that have been preserved in the Public Records Office are mainly those covering map production and the progress of work in the field parties. Material which gives some impression of the way of life at the time is disappointingly rare in these files. The breadth and content of the picture that I have been able to paint have thus depended to a large extent on the contributions and reminiscences of others. I have tried to place the contributions in a setting which produces a coherent image of the organisation but I am very conscious of the fact that mine is only one of many images that could have been produced.

Professor McGrath's monograph has been an extremely valuable reference for tracing the events leading to the merger of the Directorate with the Ordnance Survey as it was written when more official records were available than is the case today. I have however tried to avoid duplication and to make this book complementary to his work.

The book is written in four parts, representing four parts of a finite life: birth, youth, middle age and the final years. It seemed to me that the Directorate was the creation of the age in which it was conceived; it was heavily influenced by the attitudes of the years in which it grew up; as it grew older, it displayed an ability to adjust to changing attitudes but, eventually, there arose new political ideals, no less strongly held than those surrounding its birth but with which its continued existence was incompatible.

Those of us who were alive at the right time to experience the opportunities, the frustrations and the satisfaction that were part of working for the Directorate were indeed fortunate.

PART I

OFFSPRING OF EMPIRE,

1858–1945

Chapter 1

Imperial Responsibilities

The concept of national mapping by the State was accepted in Great Britain at the end of the eighteenth century with the creation of the Ordnance Survey. By the middle of the nineteenth century, the Survey was firmly embarked on the work and thoughts began to turn to the Empire. In 1858, the Director General received an instruction from his Minister in the War Office:

> Lord Panmure is desirous that you direct an early attention to the subject of Colonial Surveys, ascertaining as far as possible what works are in progress at the expense of Colonial Legislatures, and reporting whether it may not be possible to establish a system under which your department, with the concurrence of the Secretary of State for the Colonies, may assist in their systematic prosecution. [1]

In his next report to Parliament, the Director General recorded that:

> We have now furnished parties to almost all the principal colonies, and the applications which are still constantly being received from all quarters for sappers from this department show the value which is set upon the services of the men who have been trained in the school of the Ordnance Survey. [2]

It took the lack of adequate mapping for the Army in the Boer War to stimulate further interest in Colonial surveys. In evidence to the Royal Commission on the War in South Africa in 1903, Major E H Hills, Head of the Topographical Section, General Staff, argued that the approach to Colonial mapping was fragmented and proposed that a new central 'Department of African Mapping' should be charged with mapping some 40–50,000 square miles a year at a cost of about £30,000. The Department would be independent of the Ordnance Survey because 'it has practically no men competent to execute a topographical survey in a wild or tropical country.' [3]

Hills' proposal was not adopted but his successor, Major C F Close, was able to take forward the less ambitious concept of a Colonial Survey Committee in August 1905. The introduction to its first Annual Report clearly states its belief in the value of good mapping:

> Maps are necessary to define the exact limits of national territory, to show the areas and villages under the rule of native chiefs; they are essential for land registration and settlement, for the allotment of mining and forest concessions, and for the organization of internal communications.
>
> Of their necessity in war the experiences of the army in South Africa afford an eloquent testimony, and even the conduct of a 'small war' or a police expedition is much simplified by the existence of reliable maps of the scene of operations. [4]

The Committee had some effect on the production of 1:250,000 mapping in its first decade but the First World War and the economic difficulties that followed reduced its influence. Surveying activities were confined to the immediate necessities of defining land ownership while geodesy, the science concerned with the shape of the earth itself – with its regional as opposed to national benefits – was virtually abandoned.

By contrast, at home, the Ordnance Survey had, since its inception, been an impressive and successful example of a well-planned and scientifically based approach to national mapping. Its first task, on its creation in 1791, was not, as many still believe, to map Great Britain but rather to carry out a triangulation to establish the size and shape of the nation. The mapping followed on from this and had the advantage of being based on an accurate framework. The Royal Engineers officers who provided the scientific and managerial expertise were strong believers in the value of this approach and they thought that Britain should apply the same principles to its Colonies.

In 1928, the future Director General of Ordnance Survey, Brigadier H St J Winterbotham, was asked to undertake an Empire tour to assess the state of the various Survey Departments. In his Final Report, he complained of 'the lack of progress in triangulation and mapping, and the failure to organise on economical and mass-production lines'. British East and Central Africa had some of the poorest mapping and the triangulation along the Arc of the 30th Meridian, designed as early as 1906 to run from the Cape to Cairo, should be completed as quickly as possible. [5]

In the light of Winterbotham's comments, the Colonial Survey Committee, with the strong support of the War Office, succeeded in persuading the East African territories, in 1931, to fund a party of Royal Engineers under the command of Major Martin Hotine (an officer who, later in his career, was to play the central role in this story) to continue observations northwards through Tanganyika. It was not a propitious moment to restart the work as there was a serious financial crisis at home and, in 1933, the joint funding arrangements collapsed and the team and its expertise were dispersed, having advanced the triangulation up to the southern border of Ruanda Urundi, then a Belgian mandate

Seeking to increase the influence of the Committee, Winterbotham succeeded in bringing into membership several eminent geodesists who were Fellows of the Royal Society. As a result, the Royal Society itself took up the question of geodesy in the Colonies. Meanwhile, Brigadier M N MacLeod, Winterbotham's successor as Director General of the Ordnance Survey, in a paper to the Empire Survey Officers' Conference in London in 1935, appealed for Government recognition:

> Let us try to get [the Government] to accept the principle of *Imperial* responsibility for this important science, however slight the expression they decide to give it, for it is the Imperial Government alone which can coordinate the efforts of those concerned.[6]

In April 1936, the Royal Society pointed out to the Government's Economic Advisory Council:

> . . . the great economic importance of making geodetic surveys on the ground that such surveys are the foundation of all schemes of large scale development or mapping, and . . . that, especially in East Africa, the responsibility does not rest on one Territory, because the geodetic framework should be planned on geographical rather than on political lines.[7]

The next three years saw desultory consultation take place between the Colonial Office, the War Office and the Committee. Colonel P K Boulnois, the Officer Commanding the Geographical Section, General Staff (GSGS), offered a small military team who would take fifty years to complete the work. He saw it as a useful, permanent training exercise and was keen to maintain control.

MacLeod, on the other hand, felt that the Ordnance Survey was the obvious organisation to exercise technical management even if the personnel came from the Army.

After attempts had been made to obtain funding from the Royal Geographical Society and the Royal Society, the Colonial Office asked Boulnois, in early 1939, to prepare a five-year plan, to include locations, estimated progress and costs of the proposed Royal Engineers survey party. This would support an application to the Colonial Development Fund. When MacLeod persisted in his view that the Ordnance Survey should be given responsibility for supervision of Colonial surveys, Boulnois was infuriated and reminded him of his own involvement in GSGS:

> I see no reason at all why you, who carried out the duties of Chief of the Geographical Section General Staff according to the lines of policy which you found when you first occupied that chair, should wish to alter the whole position of that Section now that you have left it. You handed over certain responsibilities *vis-à-vis* the Colonial Office, and more particularly as regards getting R.E. officers trained in survey, and, unless I abrogate the whole position of the Geographical Section, I see no alternative but to follow quite exactly in your footsteps. [8]

The Committee referred the dispute to a small group, chaired by Sir Gerald Lenox-Conyngham FRS, a respected geodesist, and with Boulnois, Calder Wood (Boulnois' assistant at GSGS) and MacLeod as members. Their report left the detailed arrangements and technical instructions in the hands of GSGS, a recommendation with which MacLeod strongly disagreed. Despite the worsening situation in Europe, MacLeod and Boulnois continued to argue over where control should lie. In a letter to Boulnois on 22 August 1939, MacLeod wrote:

> . . . the policy of supervising Colonial Surveys from the War Office came into operation as a matter of pure expediency rather than as a matter of thought-out policy . . . The initiation of a [new] policy, if approved, should be, in my view, the occasion for a change in the present arrangements, because the direction of such a policy involves looking fifty or a hundred years ahead. If it is entrusted to anyone in this country at all, he should be the principal survey authority, i.e. the Director General of the Ordnance Survey, and not the officer i/c G.S.G.S., because constitutionally the officer i/c G.S.G.S. is a Staff Officer responsible to

the Army Council, and it is the Army Council only who can entrust the direction of anything to him. From the point of view of the Colonial Survey Committee or any outside body, it is unconstitutional to tell the Army Council what they consider one of their officers ought to do. [9]

Both protagonists tried to get Lenox-Conyngham to support their own point of view. Boulnois was adamant that no survey team would be made available if he did not retain control of it. [10] MacLeod, however, was hoping for some compromise agreement when he wrote to Lenox-Conyngham on 26 August, using a topical turn of phrase:

> I am still hopeful it may be possible to convert him to our opinions, as I think it may be difficult, perhaps impossible, to secure a change in the present system in the face of his opposition . . . I hope it may be possible to persuade Boulnois to agree to our views, not perhaps in the Hitlerian, but in the Halifaxian, manner. [11]

Lenox-Conyngham wanted to avoid any clear recommendation on control, preferring to concentrate on gaining approval in principle first. As late as 30 August 1939, MacLeod was still pursuing the argument:

> If Boulnois insists that our Sub-Committee's report should include recommendations about control, it will have to record disagreement between its members and presumably to give reasons for this, in which case I must say I think he will find it difficult to justify the statement that an R.E. party would be of no use unless he controls it.
>   . . . This little affair fortifies me in my opinion that if we are to get on with this and other survey jobs, the paramount necessity is to have one, and only one, authority controlling the executive work. [12]

Four days later, Britain was at war and the debate was suspended. Considerations of Colonial matters were put on hold as the military took over control of all survey and mapping facilities in pursuance of the war effort. Thus, the campaign for recognition of British Imperial responsibilities, pursued for so long by Winterbotham, MacLeod and their allies, came to a halt for reasons quite outside their control. Having finally gained acceptance of the principle of Imperial responsibility, the main players must have been dis-appointed that they were unable, in the time available to them, to settle the consequential disputes over personal fiefdoms.

Chapter 2

Wartime Visions

In the early days of the War, relationships between MacLeod and Boulnois deteriorated still further and MacLeod convinced his superiors that a new man was needed at GSGS. Colonel Martin Hotine arrived there in late 1941 and brought an immediate improvement in relations. At the same time, the Colonial Secretary was forming a Committee on Post-War Problems under the chairmanship of Lord Hailey. One of Hailey's first acts was to request a memorandum from MacLeod and Calder Wood on how the triangulation framework in Africa might be completed after the War was over. It was felt that this would be a particularly favourable moment to do the work as resources would be available and 'the circumstances at the time might render international co-operation rather easier than is generally the case.'[1] The Colonial Office accepted that Britain would take a leading part in this continental project, reflecting the prevalent Imperial view of the Nation's responsibilities.

Hotine soon expressed his view to MacLeod that the Ordnance Survey should take over the responsibility for all Colonial surveys commissioned by the Imperial Government, with GSGS acting as an 'agent' and supplying the necessary personnel. He believed that the Ordnance Survey could provide, more reliably than the military, the continuity that was needed. Thus prompted, MacLeod suggested to the Colonial Office that the Director General should become its 'Technical Adviser' in place of the Chief of GSGS, in order to encourage a more systematic approach to the work 'over many years and perhaps indefinitely', and that it should prepare a long-term plan for the work and then be responsible for its execution. Hotine responded by warning strongly against the use of Ordnance Survey personnel if they had no experience outside the mother country:

> If . . . the Ordnance Survey were to become a purely civil organisation
> [and if] in these circumstances, Ordnance Survey officers were to be
> recruited from civilians straight from the Oxford and Cambridge cradles,

whose whole horizon was included in this country, then I do not think
that Colonial Survey Departments or the Colonial Office would be
prepared to accept either their advice or their temporary services. One can
see in these circumstances that the only officers available to the Ordnance
Survey in time would be the less adventurous spirits from Oxford and
Cambridge who had fought shy of Colonial Survey employment in the
first place. The effect on the Ordnance Survey itself would, of course, be
still more disastrous and I imagine this will constitute a sufficient
safeguard. [2]

In a handwritten postscript so typical of his energetic style, he went
further and now questioned the standing of the Director General
himself amongst Colonial surveyors:

. . . if he is the 'best qualified authority' on general surveying, he didn't
get that way on prolongations and extensions [methods of urban survey
used by Ordnance Survey], with the occasional use of a chain. Colonial
Surveys at any rate won't accept the view that the head of a Dept with
obviously specialised problems is for that reason necessarily the chap to
advise them; and I am afraid that too much insistence on that view will
alienate them. [3]

The Colonial Office nevertheless invited MacLeod and Calder
Wood 'to prepare a general scheme on the basis of centralised
direction by the Colonial Office and on the assumption that reasonable financial provision will be forthcoming'. [4] In September 1942,
they recommended that the Ordnance Survey should be responsible
for such work, on behalf of the Colonial Office, once peace arrived.
They outlined the ideal way of mapping a Colonial territory, and the
difficulties that would be encountered when development schemes
were in urgent need of maps and could not wait for the lengthy
process of establishing geodetic frameworks. East and Central Africa
and the West Indies were suggested as the first-priority areas. They
defined in broad terms the size and shape of the organisation but
urged the need to take a longer view:

It may be remarked, at the outset, that it would not be worth while
creating any organisation except with the definite intention of carrying
out systematically a well thought-out programme extending over a period
of at least twenty years. This is only another way of saying that Colonial
Surveys, like those of Great Britain or India, ought to be handled by a

properly organised, permanent service, and the eventual formation of
such a service which can keep up to date any maps prepared, and maintain
and develop the surveys progressively as economic development takes
place, should be kept in mind from the beginning, however modest the
start may be. [5]

There was strong support for the use of aerial photographic methods
and it was suggested that any Air Survey Unit set up for the
Ordnance Survey could be used on Colonial work for around nine
months of the year when conditions at home were unfavourable.

Meanwhile, the Colonial Office asked MacLeod whether the
transfer of the role of adviser could not proceed immediately since all
were agreed that it should happen. MacLeod wrote to Hotine to seek
his view and received a somewhat irritated reply:

Since it has been agreed by everyone directly concerned that you, and not
I, should in future advise the Colonial Office, I should have thought all
that remained to be done was for the Colonial Office to ask you for some
advice i.e., get on with it.

If, however, the Colonial Office consider the whole matter should be
put on an exalted plane – despite the paper shortage – then I suggest they
write to the Fish and Chip shop [Ministry of Agriculture and Fisheries]
asking respectfully if their trusted servant may give them the benefit of his
advice. There is not, I suggest, any need to ask the Army Council if they
will please instruct me to desist; since I cannot discover that the Army
Council were ever asked to lay on advice from G.S.G.S. or M.I.4. or the
Officer who provided maps of the Crimea. [6]

In another handwritten postscript, he returns to the question of the
Director General's competence to act as an adviser, in a remarkably
outspoken manner for a Colonel writing to a Major General:

You will remember that the agreement was based on the assumption that
DG OS would continue to be a military officer. The Colonies will simply
not listen to advice from a DG who has passed the whole of his service at
Southampton (or Esher) and whose survey experience is confined to this
country . . . If you have not already made this clear to [the Colonial
Office], I suggest you do so. I regard it as an essential condition. [7]

MacLeod dutifully reported Hotine's view to the Colonial Office and
suggested that it should in future approach the Ordnance Survey for
advice on survey matters. The Colonial Office accepted his proposal.

Hotine's views continued to develop. He told the Colonial Survey and Geophysical Committee in November 1942 that a centralised service should:

> . . . provide facilities for the rapid transfer of survey parties and their
> equipment from one Colony to another, so that, for example, during
> periods which were climatically unsuitable for surveying operations, the
> surveyor and his instruments could be quickly transferred to some other
> area where his services could continue to be used. [8]

It is clear that Hotine was now thinking of a large organisation whose surveyors would be highly mobile. He had, at times, found the Ordnance Survey inflexible in its response to changing military requirements during the previous twelve months. He must have begun to doubt its suitability for controlling the dynamic, rapid-response organisation that he had in mind.

Parallel discussions were taking place at this time about a possible single national mapping authority. It was felt that a single authority would concentrate expertise, avoid duplication and lead to greater efficiency. Hotine thought that such an authority would be a satisfactory home for the central Colonial unit. During the discussions, a problem arose in General Headquarters, Iraq which Hotine felt could not be adequately and easily handled by someone of his relatively junior rank. He asked MacLeod if he would undertake a tour of the area to address these difficulties but MacLeod refused, saying that he had no authority to intervene in War Office matters. Hotine believed that MacLeod had missed a great chance of achieving a *de facto* acceptance of a unified authority:

> . . . this insistence on retiring into the O.S. shell will, I am afraid, wreck
> any contribution you might make towards post-war planning on Imperial
> lines. The flesh and blood of a post-war Imperial Survey organisation are
> to be found not in Southampton or Esher, but spread throughout theatres
> of war; and a D.G.O.S. who had nothing to do with them during the war
> will cut no ice on their post-war employment. The Colonies will not
> listen to you, and the vision of centralized Imperial Surveys – like the
> vision of centralized Military Surveys – will go the way of all pipe-
> dreams. [9]

He went on to chide MacLeod, in as outspoken a manner as ever, about the anxiety he felt at the idea of leaving his post to go on tour:

It is, of course, a common human failing to suppose that our deputies and successors can never achieve our own level. The last four Directors General of the Ordnance Survey seem to have been particularly afflicted that way. If they all were right, the job must about be due to be held by a cumulative mental defective. It is simpler to assume they are all wrong; including, if I may say so, yourself. [10]

Whilst both wanted to see a unified authority, MacLeod thought that DG OS should become its head *ex officio*. Hotine now saw the Ordnance Survey as a very reliable production unit but doubted its capability for improvisation and innovation. He was strongly against the idea of an *ex officio* appointment and wanted a new central headquarters unit with the Ordnance Survey as just one of a number of production units under its command. This inability to agree over the national authority was delaying a final decision about the Colonial unit and Hotine was worried about the effect of the delay on future prospects for his wartime surveyors:

[The question of Colonial Surveys] worries me personally quite a lot. We have lured into the Service a number of good chaps who look on me as their godfather and who cheerfully go anywhere and do anything I tell them. They will inevitably come to me (or my successor) after the Armistice and ask what the next job is; and I simply cannot face them with the bland statement that they are no longer my responsibility; – I (or my successor) have no suggestions to make because I handed over all peace-time surveys in the Empire to a bird known as D.G.O.S., whom they consider a cross between John Bartholomew and the Surveyor General of <u>one</u> of the 'Colonies'. The O.S. won't offer them employment and most of them wouldn't anyway smell at a bowler hat and a chain, with nothing nearer the bush than the New Forest. Unless we have a cut-and-dried means of switching war surveys to productive work in the Empire, there will be widespread unemployment in spite of the certainty of plenty of work crying out to be done. What, bar writing memoranda, is being done to prepare for this? The question will solve itself if we get complete centralization. But if we do not, then I think that Colonial Surveys must return to G.S.G.S. for the good and sufficient reason that no-one else has the threads or the machinery to handle them. They will however be properly handled this time by a machine which has organized entirely similar jobs over half the globe during the war; and production arising from them can be farmed out to O.S. exactly as it is done now. [11]

After further discussions, MacLeod asked the War Office to accept responsibility for a new national authority but the idea was rejected because of the serious risks of dislocation posed by such a major reorganisation in wartime. This brought Hotine round to the view that the institutional difficulties in the way of one Ministry acting on behalf of one or even two others were insuperable. It followed that a unit that carried out Colonial surveys should come under the sole direction of the Colonial Office. He wrote a withering response when a paper, prepared by MacLeod for consideration by the Colonial Research Committee, was circulated for comment in February 1943.

Although the paper included MacLeod's plea for a long-term organisation spanning twenty years and his own for a mobile force able to move quickly from one colony to another, it assumed Ordnance Survey control and Hotine was not satisfied. If the new organisation was to take over all trigonometric and topographic surveys in the Colonies, he argued, how could they possibly go to Colonial Governors and suggest that four officers and eight soldiers could cure the problem? – these resources were less than Nigeria had allocated to work in that Colony alone before the War. He mocked the large size of the proposed Headquarters unit in comparison to the number of field staff they were to control. He complained that no thought had been given to the plight of Colonial employees return-ing from the War to find their work removed to a central organisa-tion and suggested that, to a Colonial eye, it might appear that 'some Department at Home has an eye on its post-war stature, which it is prepared to increase at the expense of the Colonies. To this extent only can the proposal be said to have anything to do with "Empire Building".'[12]

He then suggested that the way forward was to get the principle of a central organisation accepted by the Secretary of State for the Colonies; to design a central department so as to absorb at least all the personnel who were employed on such work before the War; to work out conditions of service; and to 'get it all done before Peace breaks out so that we can at once start building it up as the Army demobilises'.[13]

His views were persuasive and a sub-committee of the Colonial Survey and Geophysical Committee, with MacLeod's successor, Major General G Cheetham, and Hotine among the members, was given the task of producing the final scheme. It was ready by March 1944 and its most significant conclusions were:

- Orderly development requires accurate mapping but mapping takes time and offers little in the way of short-term benefit. It is therefore not popular with Colonial Governments.
- Accurate mapping needs a firm regional geodetic framework if subsequent adjustments are to be avoided.
- A central organisation would allow maximum use of manpower and aerial survey resources as they could be moved to avoid seasonal delays caused by weather.
- The central organisation would concentrate on geodetic and topographical work, leaving Colonial Departments to concentrate on cadastral work.
- The Colonial Empire had an extent of around 2,250,000 square miles of which only around 400,000 square miles had been mapped. 16,000 miles of primary triangulation chain needed observing, whilst an area of 1,750,000 square miles needed secondary triangulation control.
- The organisation should have its own Air Survey Unit or, failing that, make use of RAF resources.
- Maps should be produced at scales of 1:125,000, 1:50,000 or 1:25,000, depending on the degree of development of an area. Printing should be contracted out to the Ordnance Survey.
- The organisation should be under the control of a Director General reporting to the Colonial Secretary and should be staffed by officers transferred or seconded by Colonial Departments, the Royal Engineers or the Ordnance Survey and by direct recruitment.
- In order to complete the geodetic work and 50 per cent of the outstanding topographical mapping in a space of ten years, 73 surveyors would be needed and an annual budget of £244,000.
- The prospect of having the work financed from Imperial funds would make the proposals attractive to Colonial Governments and would outweigh any feelings of damaged pride caused by giving up some traditional responsibilities. [14]

The Colonial Research Committee recommended the scheme to the Colonial Secretary, who sent it to Colonial Governors for comment. The general level of support was sufficient to allow the Colonial Secretary to approve the proposals in September 1945. In so doing, he brought to a successful end forty years of lobbying by prominent geodesists and land surveyors for a responsible Imperial approach to the mapping of the Colonies. At the same time, he created a unique opportunity for an unusual, exciting and stimulating career for some two thousand individuals who were to work in the new Directorate over the next forty years.

As a result of the passage of the Colonial Development and Welfare Act in February 1945, £2 million over ten years was made available for a Geodetic and Topographic Survey of the Colonies and, on 11 March 1946, the Directorate of Colonial (Geodetic and Topographical) Surveys came into being. It was natural that the Colonial Secretary should appoint, as its first Director, Brigadier Martin Hotine, the man who had fought so outspokenly and with such energy for the creation, in one form or another, of a central organisation.

PART II

YOUTHFUL ENERGY AND A CLEAR PURPOSE,

1946–1955

Chapter 3

Hotine's Private Army

When, on 11 March 1946, Brigadier Martin Hotine took up residence in an American Army camp in Bushy Park, Teddington, he had not only to create a new organisation from scratch but also to inject the sense of commitment and urgency which he felt so strongly himself. To help him, he was joined by Lieutenant Colonel G J Humphries (Deputy Director), Lieutenant Colonel W D C Wiggins and Group Captain J Bussey (Assistant Directors), an administrator seconded from the Colonial Office and two clerks. The service officers had all known each other well during the war years and Humphries had been in charge of the Planning Section which had designed the organisation.

Hotine, Humphries and Wiggins led the Directorate for seventeen years until Hotine's retirement. They became a powerful team, knowledgeable about the needs of the territories they served, passionate about the value of the mapping that they were providing and adept at arguing the case for funding. As time went on, the organisation became known in the corridors of Whitehall as 'Hotine's Private Army'. Indeed, Hotine had much of the freedom of an Army commander. He was given an agreed sum of money and left to decide how to spend it in the best interests of his customers. He had even more freedom because it was difficult for generalists in the Colonial Office to judge the outcome of the annual 'campaign'. Fortunately, in Hotine they had a Director committed to getting results. In a letter written a few years later, he shows that he was well ahead of his time in understanding the importance of meeting customers' needs:

> . . . the jobs exist to be done and do not exist for the purpose of employing people. This is a widespread delusion these days, but it is nevertheless a delusion. Not even a Government can continue for long to run any organisation unless its products are wanted and are delivered. [1]

23

Hotine took the appointment even though, by so doing, he gave up a strong chance of promotion to Major General in the Army. This was very much an indication of the man he was. Impatient with bureaucracy, insistent on getting things done, uninhibited in expressing his views when he believed that things were not being done properly, he commanded the greatest respect from those for whom he worked and from those who worked for him. In this new Colonial unit, he would have seen the opportunity to create an organisation committed to getting results with a sense of urgency and in pursuit of a purpose – the development of the Colonies – which he thought worthwhile. Red tape would be kept to a minimum and employees would be expected to share his enthusiasm for the work.

In the early years, Humphries and Wiggins (who had been promoted to Deputy Director in 1948) interchanged duties, taking turn and turn about on short assignments based in Nairobi. As time went on, they both settled into HQ posts and split the responsibilities between them – Humphries looking after the field surveyors overseas and Wiggins the map-production processes at home. This was a fortunate arrangement, for Humphries was the wiser and Wiggins the sharper of the two. While Humphries was intolerant of lazy surveyors, he could take their more idiosyncratic behaviour with a phlegmatic resignation. For instance, on a tour of Africa on which he had had to deal with some surveyor's errant behaviour, he remarked with a sigh: 'Macdonald, if I was granted one wish, I would have the lot of you castrated!'

Wiggins, on the other hand, was more conscious of his dignity and could be quite fierce with his staff. A twenty-nine-year-old cartographer was summoned to his office on achieving his first promotion after five years' service and told:

> I have to say that I am very unsure about this promotion. You are very young for it, you lack experience and you can consider yourself very lucky that there were so few good candidates. You will have to work extremely hard to justify your new rank. [2]

He often treated his Chief Cartographer, L D Carmichael, in a similarly abrasive fashion when setbacks were encountered. Carmichael was a man of strong principles and did much to set the standard of cartography at the Directorate. He served under Wiggins for eighteen years but things improved somewhat when the latter, who may have had some inkling of the effect of his expressions of irritation, decided to recruit a personal assistant. This role fell to a young geography graduate who was required to act as a go-between:

> One of the main jobs for which Wiggins wanted an assistant was as a
> buffer, not so much to protect himself but to protect others from his fierce
> tongue – though he probably would not have seen it quite like that. Soon
> after I arrived, Wiggins came into my office and said 'Ring up that idiot Z
> at the Hydrographic Office and tell him he is being a fool.' I was too new
> to dare to disobey and I sat for ages staring at the phone and trying to
> pluck up the courage to ring Z. Eventually I did so. A week or two later, I
> had to make my first visit to the hydrographers at Cricklewood and met
> Z. He put his elderly arm round me and said 'I'm so glad you've come to
> DCS. Do you know? – your predecessor rang me up the other week and
> told me I was a fool!' And I was hypocrite enough not to say a word. [3]

To carry out the work required, Hotine needed a workforce representing some unusual occupations:

- surveyors willing to live an itinerant life in arduous conditions in a variety of countries;
- mathematicians with the specialist experience to carry out the complex calculations of geodetic triangulation. They were always known as 'computers', a description which would cause some confusion on the advent of electronic computers;
- photogrammetrists, a new breed of expert in the art of making maps from aerial photography;
- cartographers able to prepare the final drawings of the maps themselves.

This amounted to a requirement for 4 Directing Staff, 3 Regional Surveyors General, 81 Surveying and 151 Drawing Office Staff. The regional appointments carried the same rank as Deputy Director and were to be responsible for West Africa, East and Central Africa and the Far East and Pacific though, in the event, these posts were not filled until the 1960s when Regional Survey Officers, at Principal level, were appointed.

Recruitment was hindered by an initial inability to offer permanent employment on pensionable terms. As for the wartime Army surveyors for whom Hotine had felt such responsibility, the lure of a hard life in the bush was too unattractive after so many years separated from families and the comforts of home life. Few Colonial

surveyors shared Hotine's belief that the work of the central organisation represented the peak of professional activity. Hotine, a great
mathematician, followed in the tradition of Everest and other
prominent Fellows of the Royal Society in seeing geodesy – the
study of the shape of the earth – and map-making as the highest
challenges in land surveying. By contrast, the Colonial surveyor saw
the demarcation of individual land holdings as the truly professional
work which gave him a significant standing in the community.
Giving up both home comforts and status was too great a deterrent
and, in the event, only three transfers resulted – those of Humphries
and Wiggins from Nigeria to directing posts and the rather unusual
recruitment (for its time) of Will Young, a British Honduran citizen
with Canadian degrees, as a field surveyor. In all, only twelve
surveyors were recruited during the first year of operation and this
severely delayed the creation of overseas surveying parties.

Recruitment of cartographers also proceeded slowly and there
was a disappointingly low proportion of fully trained recruits so that
it was some time before many could be put on to productive work.
The poor terms of employment encouraged a drift to the private
sector as opportunities arose and, by the end of the first year, only
thirty-five staff were fully trained and still in post. Fortunately, there
was a small core of ex-Royal Engineers with wartime experience to
provide the expertise and to carry out the training.

These difficulties led Hotine to follow up a contact he had made in
the Free Polish Army during the War. The Polish Army had a cadre
of well-qualified Polish surveyors and cartographers awaiting resettlement at a camp in Inverary on the west coast of Scotland. He
persuaded the Colonial Office to accept their qualifications and to
issue the surveyors with papers to enable them to travel overseas.
Two Polish surveyors were selected in 1947 and a further eight in
1948. Many of them had been cut off from their families in Poland by
the Iron Curtain and, with little to keep them in Britain, were glad to
take the opportunity of an exciting job in a remote area. At the same
time, seventeen cartographers were recruited. Both groups made a
major contribution to the work of the Directorate and brought
charm and style to social gatherings at home and overseas.

From April 1948, the Colonial Office agreed to offer permanent
appointments. As a result, many of the home-based staff then
remained with the Directorate for the whole of their careers though
the celibate and itinerant life overseas continued to produce a high
level of resignations amongst surveyors.

This initial recruitment produced a workforce which broke down roughly into three equal parts: a third came from a wartime background, a third were young people straight from school and a third were a group who spoke very little English, at least to start with. It was an unusual and fairly volatile combination. The ex-servicemen were relieved to be free of the constraints of military life and took considerable delight in ignoring such rules as were intended to regulate their lives while the Poles, with their foreign accents and strange names, were a continual source of suspicion to the American Military Police who still guarded the camp. There was no formal training in English for the Poles and there were many difficulties in the early days in explaining to them what had to be done. Gradually, however, they acquired an ability to speak the language though their landladies complained that they used certain words without too clear an understanding of what exactly they meant.

A family atmosphere rapidly developed at Bushy Park. Everyone lived close by and social activities were strongly supported. The Poles, with little to occupy them in the evenings, willingly undertook to prepare sports pitches by hand digging. The wood for goalposts was acquired by pooling everyone's very limited entitlement to that scarce commodity. There was a whole range of useful services available from members of staff who had special skills or contacts: watch repairs, betting shops, carpentry, artwork. Refreshments were delivered by the head messenger who carried round twice a day two 3-gallon buckets filled with sugared tea. In his apron pocket, he carried a selection of buns and, in his back pocket, cheese rolls. Towards the end of the round, the fillings had fallen out to the bottom of his pockets and he was left with a number of plain rolls. However, to effect a sale, he was always prepared to rummage and make one up to order! It may be that not every customer was entirely satisfied for Humphries wrote to Wiggins in Nairobi: 'A spot of bother the other day when Burford set about Hall the messenger and knocked him about a bit. It has been settled amicably but Hall is still away sick.'[4] When it was discovered that the acetate film used in the drawing offices had explosive properties, a craze for building rocket-propelled boats developed. These were displayed on the ponds in the Park at lunch-times and achieved velocities – and occasionally vertical take-offs – that amazed the onlookers.

The accommodation was spartan and the first winter of 1947 was one of the coldest on record. However, there was a great feeling of excitement about being involved in what was seen as important and urgent work, using new techniques which were still relatively untried in the industry at large. Hotine assembled the staff and told them that being excellent cartographers was not enough – they needed to be imbued with the vision and the commitment to help the less well-off inhabitants of the Colonies. Wiggins was seen every day walking round the offices, talking to staff about the work, and there was little sense of demarcation. The wartime attitude of everyone working together prevailed and, when a drawing office was being established for a new influx of staff, Wiggins would arrive with a large quantity of screwdrivers and he and the cartographers would all take off their jackets and spend a morning assembling desks.

This spirit was encapsulated in 1948 by George Henlen, who became Establishment Officer in June 1947 and who had earlier been one of the Colonial Office officials involved in the planning of the Directorate. He wrote in the house magazine:

> Difficulties in the original planning and in getting the final stages of the scheme completed made [us] despair of ever getting anywhere. Indeed it is very doubtful if the organisation would have seen the light of day but for the great faith of the master mind of the planners, Brigadier Hotine, who despite his enormous responsibilities as Director of Military Surveys during the war, spent as much of his valuable time as he could at the Colonial Office pressing his arguments upon all and sundry.
>
> . . . There are still problems to solve; problems of recruitment, problems of programming, problems of equipment and stores, and above all problems of permanency and establishment for the staff . . . Let us remember the difficulties of the original believers in the scheme and let us show their patience and tenacity to see these other problems through. I feel confident . . . that all will come right soon, and we shall be able to look back on the past few months and find faith had been justified. We ourselves are the pioneers; like the Colonists of old we are breaking new ground, bringing into the Directorate some portion of the traditions of the Ordnance Survey, the Colonial Survey Service, the Directorate of Military Survey, the Royal Engineers, the Royal Air Force and the commercial firms such as Bartholomew's and Phillips. Gradually we shall develop a tradition of our own which will be in keeping with the ideals of our Director and which will weld us into an organisation to become famed throughout the Colonial Empire, and elsewhere.
>
> In building up this organisation there have been anomalies and disappointments. These I would emphasise are due to teething troubles.

In ten years time . . . anomalies will no longer concern us; in fifty years time, the traditions being built up now will be something of which our successors will be proud. We are passing through the period of trial and error into the period of achievement. Let us stand firmly together and resolve that now we have the tools, we shall see the job through. [5]

With such Churchillian enthusiasm, the Directorate embarked on a life which brought the recognition and achievement that Henlen expected even though it did not last the fifty years of which he spoke.

Chapter 4
The Tools for the Job

In 1946, Hotine had undertaken to map 900,000 square miles in the Colonies within ten years and intended to do this using aerial photography. This was a relatively new method of mapping for which he had done considerable research in his younger days but which had not been widely used in Great Britain until the war. The technique, known as photogrammetry, made several novel demands on the technologies of the day:

- The aerial photography had to be flown along precise flight lines from a height of 15,000 to 20,000 feet, so that both successive photographs in a strip and adjacent strips over-lapped. The overlap between adjacent photographs could then be seen in three dimensions when viewed stereoscopically in the Drawing Office.
- Surveyors in the field had to establish the positions of points of detail on the ground which could be clearly and precisely identified on the photographs. These would allow the accurate scaling and positioning of the photographs.
- Photogrammetrists could then use machines to view the three-dimensional model of the ground surface, scale it and plot the required information.
- Cartographers would draw the maps from this information.

An agreement was made with the Ordnance Survey, and later with the Military Survey Service, to print the maps but the Directorate employed its own photographers to produce the material required for the printing process.

The use of air photography for mapping had become more advanced on the Continent than in Britain due to the presence of major equipment manufacturers in Germany and Switzerland. The sophisticated machines required for these advanced processes were expensive and, although there were cheaper machines available in the United States, there was, in 1946, no significant production in

Britain. Unfortunately, at the end of the War, there were stringent controls on the purchase of foreign currency, and dollars were virtually unobtainable. Even if the Treasury had authorised a large capital investment, the foreign currency would have been impossible to obtain for purchases which were hardly essential to the well-being of the population.

Hotine had, however, been responsible for the development of simple low-cost techniques before the War and these were quickly adopted. Scaling and positioning of the photographs were to be achieved by the strange rite of 'Slotted Template Assembly'. This required the construction of a large, stable and carefully levelled wooden floor. The wood was painted and an accurate rectangular grid of co-ordinates was then carefully set out on the surface. Each photograph was represented by a plastic template into which several radial slots had been cut by a specially constructed machine. Using a collection of studs, the overlapping templates could be joined together. The surveyors' identified control points were plotted on the board beforehand and studs pinned down to the board in those positions. This provided overall scale and small local variations could be accommodated by movement along the slots. Movement could be assisted by the judicious use of a rubber hammer so that the templates were all lying flat. Then the floating studs connecting individual photographs were pinned to the board, the assembly lifted and the co-ordinates of the pins measured. These co-ordinates were used to provide the precise position and scale of individual photographs during the plotting process.

Not everything went to plan – the paint first applied to the surface was deficient in some way and a new eighteen-year-old recruit was horrified to find it coming off complete with the carefully marked grid when he was set to washing it clean one day. He was marched into Hotine's office in a state of shock by his Superintendent but fortunately the Director applied his wrath to the Works Department. The floor was a holy place and all staff working on it were required to remove their shoes and wear specially made felt slippers. Not everyone got the message, however: one youngster was working on the floor when his Superintendent cautioned him to take care not to tread on the pins sticking out of the studs. 'Don't worry, sir! I've got a really strong pair of boots on and they won't get through these soles.' Unfortunately, the roof was supported by a series of concrete pillars and these meant that large assemblies had to be laid round them, leaving small holes in the laydown. Careful thought had to be given to any new job to ensure that a critical control point did not fall in one of these holes.

The plotting of detail was an equally laborious process, using hand stereocopes to view the three-dimensional model and a multitude of coloured poster paints to mark the detail that was to be copied onto the final map. A complex procedure was necessary to compensate for the distortions on the photographs caused by ground relief. The work was repetitive and needed concentration and care but there was scope for innovation and flexibility:

> This was the kind of thing which made DOS so unique. We were always ready to do the unconventional, to bend the method. These methods could be clumsy and sometimes had an element of the Heath Robinson about them but they were cheap and practical and we mapped thousands of square miles quickly as a result. Besides being able to turn our hands to any cartographic process, we were also expected to know the details of the country which we were mapping. I became so informed on Uganda at one stage that a visitor from Jinja asked me when I had lived out there. [1]

Hotine was determined that the mapping of the Colonies should be based on a sound survey framework of geodetic and secondary triangulation. A triangulation started from a datum position on the earth's surface determined by a series of astronomical observations. A base-line of around ten miles in length was measured in a conveniently flat area and this was then connected to a series of triangles formed by hilltop stations at suitable intervals. After all the angles had been measured, spherical trigonometry could be used to calculate the latitudes and longitudes of the individual stations. The surveyors needed expensive theodolites for this work and even British models were in short supply.

The field work would be very weather dependent and the surveyors would need to move from country to country to avoid the rainy season. They therefore had to be very mobile and so were to be provided with all the essential items of camp life – from canvas wash basins to meat skewers and from teaspoons to soda siphons. The latter may have reflected the Directing trio's enthusiasm for pink gin just as the six place-settings of crockery and cutlery that were provided for each man might have reflected the Director's hospitable nature. Three special boxes were provided to carry this kitchen equipment though their size and weight soon brought them into disfavour with local porters. A field desk was designed in wood and

1 Brigadier Hotine, Director (right) and Colonel Humphries, Deputy Director, discussing surveyor movements on the latter's famous wall–map of Africa in 1957. *Crown copyright*

2 W D C Wiggins, Deputy Director (right) with Group Captain J Bussey, Assistant Director, in 1957. *Crown copyright*

3 D E Warren, Director 1968–1980, discussing a training exercise with F A Obiamiwe, a cartographer from the Federal Survey Department of Nigeria on a training attachment to the Directorate, 1968. *Crown copyright*

4 B E Furmston, Director 1980–1984 (centre), with Princess Sirindhorn of Thailand, herself a qualified photogrammetrist, and L Bryant, 1980. *Crown copyright*

5 Fred Gaselee, the Superintendent of Training, explains the intricacies of map projections to young cartographers, in 1954. *Crown copyright*

6 The largest Slotted Template Assembly laid down at Tolworth. Constructed in 1952, it covered fifty-six 1:50,000 map sheets of Tanganyika (H Luckett and A E Fevyer kneeling). *Crown copyright*

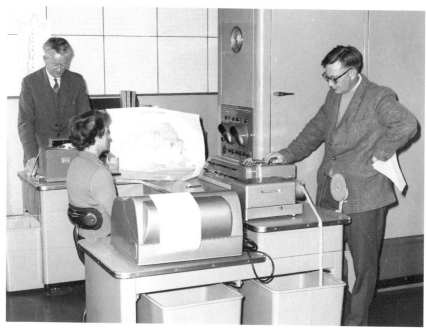

7 Harry Brazier, Chief Computer 1947–1972 (right), Lucia Windsor and Jock Watson using the Ferranti Pegasus computer at Military Survey, Feltham in 1960. *Crown copyright*

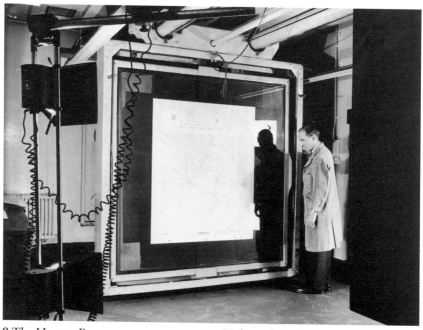

8 The Hunter Penrose process camera at Tolworth in 1954 with M Kowal, a photographer. The copyboard was large enough to allow complete map components to be photographed during the reproduction process. *Crown copyright*

9 A roomful of Kern PG2 plotting machines with S R Munn in the foreground. These machines were the mainstay of the photogrammetric production process during the 1970s. *Crown copyright*

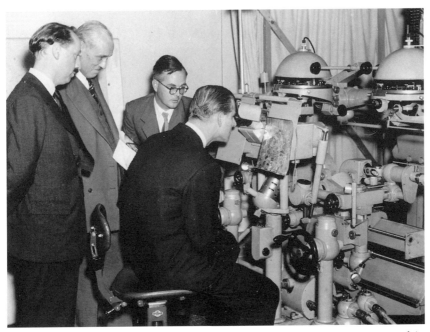

10 HRH the Duke of Edinburgh visited the Tolworth HQ in 1953 and is seen here sampling a view of Africa on a Zeiss C5 plotting machine. Looking on (left to right) are Vic Williams, Assistant Chief Cartographer, Brigadier Hotine, Director and William Jenkinson, Higher Grade Draughtsman. *Crown copyright*

11 Alastair Macdonald (the author) and Harry Green relaxing in their base accommodation – a redundant operating theatre – in Bamenda, Southern Cameroons, 1958. *A S Macdonald*

12 Planning the next day's work – Chris Bere (far left), the party leader in 1962, holds a conference in his tent near Moshi, Tanganyika with (clockwise) Musyoka Masundi, Jim Bollard, George Godon, ?, Capt Noel Charles RE, Elias, Francis Ndaga and Anton Kioko. A travelling field desk in the centre of the photograph. *Crown copyright*

13 Cooks preparing breakfast for a survey party during a move from Kenya to Tanganyika, 1950. *P J Taylor*

14 During the rains, camp conditions could be unpleasant – a flooded camp-site at Ijara, Kenya in 1976. *S H Mason*

15 Porters crossing a flooded river on the Gold Coast in 1951. Much was expected of porters and, while there were often arguments about what was and was not reasonable, there were always men like these ready to take on a challenge just for the sake of it. *P J Taylor*

16 Porters crossing a river on the Lake Shore of Nyasaland in 1960. *Crown copyright*

aluminium, with compartments to take foolscap files, and this was much more successful, retaining its popularity throughout the life of the Directorate.

The shopping list was a long one and post-war shortages were compounded by a bureaucratic embargo by the Treasury on all purchases until it was decided how they might be made. Eventually, the Ministry of Supply was authorised to proceed on the Director-ate's behalf but its experience was not well suited to the purchase of the small quantities and unusual items that were needed. Frustrated by a lack of progress, Wiggins took to putting on his Army uniform, commandeering a one-ton truck and touring Army stores depots. At each depot, by his own account:

> I drew any stores I could find that seemed suitable and signed for them. I never enquired what accounting took place over these transactions. Once I found a disused cotton mill full of 100 000 brand new 5″ heliographs (shades of the Boer War!) and drew a modest 50 – in the light of hindsight I should have quadrupled the number. [2]

Heliographs are sets of small mirrors whose angle to the sun can be controlled very accurately. This allows them to be seen over distances of up to 80 miles as a smaller version of the sun. They were originally produced for signalling purposes but, to surveyors, they are invaluable as targets for angular measurement between distant hill tops. They were made to an extremely high standard and, by the 1950s, were too expensive to copy, so the Directorate, in its later years, suffered from dwindling and well-worn stocks.

Wiggins tracked down another warehouse full of theodolites as well as a few plotting machines of Continental manufacture, which had come to Britain as War reparations. These were assembled by the staff, who taught themselves as they went along, and were used for special tasks at larger scale in, for instance, the West Indies. These complicated and beautifully made machines bestowed great status on their operators who formed an elite group, set apart from the rest like acolytes in a shrine.

Some Zeiss Multiplex plotting equipment was acquired in this way but British equipment made by Williamson was ordered and, in the first year, sixty-five projectors were delivered. Their main use was for contouring. In such equipment, two adjacent photographs are projected, through blue and red filters respectively, onto a large and solid table in a darkened room. By viewing the table through a pair of spectacles with red and blue lenses, the operator sees a three-dimensional model on which he can trace the contours. These dark rooms with solid tables offered the opportunity for many afternoon siestas unseen by supervisors. It is alleged that close encounters of a more active kind were known to take place but, whether that was the case or not, the siestas were interrupted by jealous colleagues on the outside who would place kippers in the air-cooling unit and leave them for a few days to go off. Others would blow a steady stream of small soap bubbles through a vent which, in the restricted lighting, could cause an operator who had been at a party the night before to think that he was suffering from *delirium tremens*.

Because of all the complex and expensive equipment that was being used, much of it requiring shipment overseas, carpenters and storekeepers became important members of the team. Initially, packing was a team effort, as the first Annual Report of the Directorate recorded: 'Office of Works carpenters were borrowed, old boxes were remade and the packing was done by surveyors themselves and anyone else who could be impressed.'[3] However, a carpenter, Bill Rodgers, soon arrived and stayed for thirty years. He provided a steady flow of boxes and crates for overseas parties, as well as many of the wooden tables used at Headquarters. Shipping was an unreliable business as John Mankin, a Stores Officer, recorded in a letter to a surveyor overseas:

> In the case of a shipment to the Falkland Islands I had to intervene personally at the Docks to prevent two cases being 'shut out' and you should have heard the language and threats from the stevedores when I disturbed their routine of loading but shipping to the Falklands is not so frequent and I stood my ground (the Agent kept discreetly in the background) and got them on by bribery! It is I'm afraid constant competition with these difficulties that we are faced with today and we also have to keep a close watch on impending strikes at the Docks – believe me there is always something to contend with. Mind you, I do not think it is inefficiency or mental or physical inertia on the part of those concerned – it just happens. When I was chasing one of our more important indents with the Ministry of Supply some years ago, I discovered they had calmly put it away – and so the game goes on![4]

The Directorate grew up in an era of shortages in every area of life. Lost or damaged instruments were a major cause for concern as it was not easy to replace them. Individuals were held responsible for the safe custody of their equipment and discrepancies were handled with a mix of bureaucracy and understanding. Even a solitary teaspoon lost in the bush might give rise to an assessment by the Stores Accountant: 'The Deputy Director has ruled that you were 40% to blame. Value: 6d. TO PAY: 2½d. Please make your cheque out to the Paymaster General for this amount.' One damaged theodolite received more generous treatment:

> Returning from Bechuanaland in early 1956, my mind was troubled. A dust-devil had caused the survey umbrella to knock my Geodetic Theodolite off a survey pillar and it was smashed. At that time this theodolite cost about £1000; my salary was about £750 per annum and I didn't know if I would have to pay for all or part of the damage. I needn't have worried. The stores staff at Tolworth were marvellous and I was regaled by stories of how they themselves had lost or damaged thousands of pounds worth of radar equipment, stores, etc, etc. I had nothing to pay.[5]

While applications of the rule book could appear to be petty at times, there was a refreshing willingness to dispense with it when it was in the interests of fairness to do so. The staff were encouraged by this attitude and it certainly contributed to the atmosphere that Jock Watson recalled:

> There was a zeal and enthusiasm about the work of the department. Team work and efficiency were the be-all and end-all of production; there was a *joie de vivre* about the place that was difficult to define or to attribute to any one factor; there was a wholehearted togetherness between Directors and staff, a unanimity about the ways and means of producing, as quickly as possible, accurate and much-needed maps for Colonial development.[6]

Chapter 5

First Steps Abroad

It was decided to send the first team of surveyors to the Gold Coast to provide ground control for mapping the area covered by the Volta Dam project, a scheme to provide hydro-electric power for a new bauxite industry. By November 1946, sufficient stores had been accumulated to allow the despatch of a three-man team, led by Walter Smith (who, in another thirty years, would become Director General of the Ordnance Survey). The flight out was a more leisurely journey than modern air travel as Jock Watson, a member of the team, has recorded:

> First stop was Bordeaux for coffee and fuel. Next an overnight stop in a fabulous hotel in Lisbon. The following morning, after a 4 am coach ride to the airport, we took off for Casablanca for lunch, then tea and lemon juice on the Rio de Oro at a desert airstrip complete with tents, Arabs and camels and, of course, thousands of flies buzzing round the tea. Onward to Bathurst in the Gambia and its perforated metal landing strip, to spend an uproarious night as guests of the R.A.F. The third day was comparatively sedate with a stop for lunch at Freetown, Sierra Leone and then touchdown at Accra airport in the early afternoon. [1]

With no prior experience available, assumptions had to be made about the best arrangements for efficient working. The first party leaders suffered considerable frustration as they sought to modify these arrangements to achieve greater efficiency and to respond to the pressure to get quick results so that the increasing number of cartographers at Headquarters could be kept in productive work.

Perhaps unavoidably, the initial policy was to rely heavily on collaboration with and support from the Survey Department of the Colony in question. Humphries' instructions to Smith on departure were quite explicit:

> From the time you land in the Gold Coast you and your party will come under the direct control of the Director of Surveys, Gold Coast, and you

will carry out any instructions issued by him. He will supply you with
African surveyors to assist in your work, also with the necessary
headman, chainmen and survey labourers. Any communications to this
Directorate will be made through the Director of Surveys, Gold Coast. [2]

However, the under-staffed Department was unable to assist
Smith in the secondment of sufficient experienced personnel and he
became a strong believer in the need for a greater degree of
independence and self-sufficiency. It had been hoped that the work
would be completed in six months but this had assumed full strength
and full efficiency from the day of arrival, an impossible dream. The
lack of assistance from the Department, a higher than expected
incidence of sickness among surveyors and delays in the provision of
aerial photography slowed the work down quite seriously so that it
was still not complete when the Volta and Afram Rivers rose to their
seasonal flood-levels in September 1947 and work in the area had to
be suspended. There were problems, too, with the quality of the
aerial photography being supplied by the RAF as Smith reported in
November 1947:

> What with bad weather, bad photography and the grass about as high as it
> can be, I am getting a little tired of trying to make something out of the
> nothing which the RAF provides. We have been levelling on the Sene
> River up to about twenty miles west of Krachi and we have not hit the
> 250ft contour. The photography is getting worse and it is difficult for the
> surveyor to find where he is, let alone find control points. Unless we
> reach [the 250ft contour] very soon, I shall have to call it off. [3]

The surveyors finally left the Gold Coast at the end of January 1948
by which time three more field parties were operating in Uganda,
Kenya and Tanganyika. The aim in Uganda was to provide mapping
of the remote area inhabited by the Karamojong along the border
with Kenya, where there was serious concern about sustaining water
supplies for the population. In Kenya, the mapping was required to
support land reform and improvement while, in Tanganyika, it was
needed for the ill-fated plan to grow ground-nuts in various parts of
the country.

Much of this work was in remote and uninhabited areas and made
considerable physical and mental demands on the surveyors concerned. They established a strong tradition of endurance and commitment. In Uganda, P M Kozlowski and Z M Studzinski, two of

the Polish recruits, went into the wild Karamoja region and stayed there for three years before they completed the work – at a time when most surveyors were returning to Britain every twelve months. Kozlowski's reports are laconic for the most part, reflecting his unfamiliarity with the language. However, this extract from his report for 1950 provides a flavour of the conditions:

> Whilst I was busy completing the primary observations, Studzinski, in the plains, was fighting the native superstitions, for the beacons were repeatedly and completely destroyed. The District Commissioner suggested that the Karamojong destroyed the beacons because the wire of which they are constructed was a big temptation to them. But, even when we started to use bark ropes, the damage very often happened so at particular stations we were forced to rebuild the beacon four times.
>
>   . . . We had trouble with transport, two donkeys of Studzinski's caravan died, and shortage of water was acute. At the end of the year, . . . Studzinski was surveying in the uninhabited Kidepo valley, where he was hindered by herds of buffalo, rhinoceros and elephant.
>
>   . . . It is hard to explain all the difficulties we had during the last year of our survey in Karamoja. [4]

At the end of their long tour, Kozlowski wrote to the East African High Commission in connection with their passages home:

> I have to inform you that we would like to go via more comfortable boat via Cape Town or Suez . . . We are also prepared as Col Humphries suggested to take two weeks of our leave in Kenya to use as preparation for our long leave in England. We spent three years in wild country very far from any town in which we could make suitable shopping. [5]

In Tanganyika, the surveyors were working in uninhabited country between Mpanda and Lake Tanganyika. B B Sandford and W H Organistka set off on a foot safari from Kigoma in early April 1948 and did not return until mid-July. In an account in the house magazine, Sandford described the trip:

> I, having obtained 35 porters from Kigoma, sailed in 'Liemba' and established the main base camp at Mgambo with *posho* [mealie meal] for two months . . . At Karogo, we had the misfortune to lose one porter who was taken by crocodile, an extremely unpleasant sight . . . We set off from Karogo on the 10th April and followed the Malagarasi through

elephant grass fifteen feet high . . . Going was extremely difficult at this stage as we were only able to follow the track for a few miles owing to the high grass and torrential rain which poured upon us daily as we followed compass bearings to Masangwe. This although only a distance of 22 miles took three days. The country was heavily forested in deep gullies which crossed our line of advance. Game was very plentiful, buffalo, hartebeest, roan, buck.

On 18th April we struck the Lugufu, a torrent of water some 40 yds in width running at 7–8 knots. Discovering a fording place for elephants, we attempted to cross in like manner but without success. I suffered many bruises when I was swept off my feet and afterwards hauled back by ropes over the rocky bottom.

We met with greater success by felling an enormous tree on the river bank further upstream to form a bridge. Great panic prevailed among the natives whilst constructing the bridge; they were in the water when half a dozen water snakes swam into their midst. This difficult operation took over six hours but fortunately it did the trick although it was swept away a minute or two after I (the last) had crossed.

The thirteen miles to Karurumpeta took two days through heavy forest and bad tsetse fly areas. Here again we had no paths other than the tracks of elephants which seemed to run in ever-decreasing circles. Having completed the reconnaissance and beaconing at Karurumpeta we moved on to Halembe, another exhausting journey during which we became lost in a deep ravine and had to cut a way out through thick undergrowth . . . We arrived on 22nd April, the boys' *posho* having been exhausted also our own food, rice and tea. Here we spent five days giving our legs a chance to recover. Recent travels had brought on bush sores and they were much inflamed and swollen . . . In the round trip covering an area of 500–600 sq mls we were in completely dead territory, no village, no population, no roads – and the whole area is like this from the Mpanda road westward to the Lake – an area of 1600 sq mls.

Throughout the return trip we suffered through the scarcity of water, poor visibility and long grass with an edge like a knife . . . I spent three days on toast and tea and finally made a desperate attempt to find some game. Eventually I felled my first buffalo – altogether a frightening experience and only surpassed by the pangs of hunger. [6]

It had been decided in 1945 that aerial photography would be taken by the RAF. A flight of six Lancasters and one Dakota from 82 Squadron was assigned to the task. The aircraft would navigate along circular arcs around radar stations established and operated by a support unit. Six radar stations were to be flown out and eight vehicles specially equipped for film processing sent out by sea. One hundred-and-eighty officers and other ranks were involved. It was a major logistical exercise to position the detachment but the high cost of the operation was justified by the stringent training that it would provide. The agreement required the Colonial Office to make a contribution, initially £25,000 per 80,000 square miles covered, to the Air Ministry.

It had been hoped that, by using two radar stations, it would be possible to fix the positions of the photographs with sufficient accuracy to allow the maps to be plotted without surveyors going on the ground but, although this was done later in Gambia, it did not turn out to be generally practicable.

As a result of the first, exploratory detachment to the Gold Coast in 1946, it was decided that the initial stages of the much larger 1947 operation in East and Central Africa justified the stationing of a Deputy Director in Nairobi to act as liaison officer. Humphries and Wiggins took it in turn to carry out this duty and it proved to be a wise decision. There were many changes of priority to be discussed with individual colonies before they were authorised and passed on to the RAF. Everyone had a view on what the weather was doing and was likely to do. The need for the utmost care in maintaining track and minimising variations in aircraft attitude was not yet fully appreciated by the pilots. The RAF wanted a fixed plan which would never change. The Directorate wanted to adjust plans to take account of changes in the weather pattern and local priorities. In the early years, with little photography in hand, it was essential to do everything possible to get sufficient work for the photogrammetric units at Headquarters.

Things did not start well as the radar tracking units arrived with many essential items missing. However, by July, Hotine was writing to RAF Benson: 'I understand that the job is going well in East Africa now. Even the pessimistic Humphries seems to be quite cheerful these days from which I suppose we may infer that it is going very well indeed.'[7]

In the first five months, photography covering 83,000 square miles was acquired and, by the end of 1948, this had risen to 295,000 square miles, in spite of major problems in getting spares and sufficient manpower.

The Fairchild K17 cameras available to the RAF were not capable of producing photography of consistently high quality unless handled with great care and the early photography proved difficult to use. The main problem lay in maintaining the necessary vacuum to keep the film completely flat at the instant of exposure. Bussey, the Assistant Director (Air), explained the effect in a contribution to the Squadron's house magazine:

> We tried to use it to depict the shape of the ground, as engineers wanted some accurate contours for the construction of a very imposing and important dam at Kariba. We are still grappling but, frankly boys, nearly beaten. Some of the photography just won't set up in the Multiplex equipment; it is like trying to carry a stack of dishes when several in the pile are warped; the result is just as disastrous and has a tendency to make the Zambezi flow backwards. [8]

Close inspection of the cameras revealed that a number of insects were living inside them. On another occasion, a member of the crew had been inadvertently stepping on the vacuum pipe, thus causing some non-existent hills and hollows to be plotted on the subsequent maps. It was not until a new camera was developed by the Royal Aircraft Establishment and manufactured by Williamson in 1953 that these problems disappeared – though others, less serious, took their place. However, the RAF contribution was certainly impressive in terms of area covered. In the first six years, they photographed over one million square miles of Africa and, as Hotine so teasingly put it in answering a question about the merits of using the RAF rather than the private sector:

> If the squadron were not used for the purpose, it would be used in the ordinary military training atmosphere of going up before lunch, taking a photograph of the airfield, coming down, developing the photograph, printing it, tearing up the print, and then having lunch. It is cheaper to employ the squadron on really productive work, and the men liked it because they could see that it was getting them somewhere. [9]

Chapter 6

Dams and Railways, Ground-nuts and Locusts

Hotine was not only Director, he was also Survey Adviser to the Secretary of State. His relationship with the Directors of Colonial Departments was thus that of *primus inter pares*. By 1948, there was a long shopping list of work to be done and a queue of Colonies jostling for position. It was his job, theoretically by 'advising' the Secretary of State, to judge the priorities and to decide the order of work. It was a role which could have given rise to much aggravation but Hotine had strong personal beliefs about working with others:

> A purist in organisation would say that one Department, and one only, must be responsible for all surveys of the same bit of ground. Four years ago I would have gone some way towards agreeing with him, with the mental reservation that such an organisation is too pure ever to have been conceived, much less born, except as a very primitive form of life. But I know now that the system of *primus inter pares* and collective responsibility can be made to work even in this severe testing ground. It requires goodwill, but without goodwill no organisation will work. It also requires a very high degree of co-operation, but without co-operation in this complex modern world nothing can be achieved. Now co-operation simply means working together and quite clearly the first step towards it is to get down to work. The next step is to have the same object in working, preferably to get the job as a whole done and done properly. You may think the other fellow has no such object. If so your best line is to assume he has, and anyway have it yourself. If we *all* did that, there would be co-operation. [1]

The fact that the Treasury had agreed to provide £2 million over the unusually long period of ten years meant that priorities could be allocated in a way which kept hope alive for those at the back of the queue. Acceptance of any delay was helped by the fact that queuing and rationing were part of life in post-war Britain. Hotine also needed to design the work programme so that there would be enough work at the various stages of the process to keep his field surveyors, photogrammetrists and cartographers fully occupied. Only in this way could he maintain the greatest possible production efficiency. Fortunately, the Directorate had taken up some mapping in the West Indies which had been controlled by Royal Engineers surveyors in 1946, in anticipation of the creation of the organisation. Some new mapping tasks were taken up in British Somaliland and West Africa using ground control from other sources and the appointment of the Directorate as the mapping agency for the Falkland Islands Dependencies Survey also helped to balance the workload. There was thus sufficient work for the cartographers from the outset, and there was time for the surveyors to make the necessary observations to provide the first consignments of ground control from the African projects.

The initial priority was to support Colonial Development and Welfare schemes which were funded under the same Act as the Directorate itself. Thus, in the first few years, mapping was provided for the abortive proposal to drive a railway from the Tanganyika coast to the Copperbelt in Northern Rhodesia (the Central African Rail Link), for the Volta, Kariba and Kafue Dams and for ground-nut and rice cultivation schemes in Tanganyika. For the survey of the Rail Link and for the Tanganyika schemes, large mobile parties of surveyors were assembled and urgency was the order of the day. Nevertheless, the Colonial governments were themselves unsure of exactly what was needed and there were constant changes of priority. This reflected the post-war search for economic development and increased agricultural production. Territories such as Tanganyika were happy hunting grounds for experts from the Overseas Food Corporation, the UN Food and Agriculture Organization, forestry institutes and mining companies. All said that mapping was an essential pre-requisite of development. Colonial governments were anxious to get the funds for any project while those funds were available and saw the lack of mapping as a barrier. As new funds became available, changes of priority occurred which led to uncertainty. The Directors tried very hard to adjust to these changes but they inevitably had an effect on production as Wiggins, who lacked Hotine's jovial approach to co-operation, pointed out in an acerbic letter to the Colonial Office:

[The Tanganyika Savingram] must have been despatched under a misapprehension. It is our policy to tell each Colony that it must sort out its own internal priorities and [give us] an agreed answer. This is to avoid a bombardment by each and every head of department; we prefer to deal with the Head of the Survey Department and indeed find that this works very well as we talk the same language.

I rather resent 'a certain number of preliminary plots have already been received . . .' In fact they have had 164 and would have had more if only they would leave us alone for a while without jumping their priorities about every year. Mapping is a long term affair and one of the biggest delaying factors is starting, and then putting on one side, area after area. Quite apart from the dislocation in the actual organisation, there is . . . the bad effect on the morale of our staff if they can never get to the end of any job. We have had so many jobs on top priority which have been shelved long before completion that the very words 'top priority' have begun to mean nothing more than 'wolf, wolf.'[2]

Changes to plan could be very wasteful. In one case in Tanganyika, 20,000 square miles of air photography, notified as a priority the local Survey Department, was obtained of the Lake Province. Before it could be put to use, other schemes had taken higher priorities and the photography was never used, much to Humphries' irritation.

Humphries had established in Tanganyika at this time the largest party that the Directorate ever assembled, thirteen in all, and managing their work was quite complex even without the changes. Frequent movements of surveyors could leave Headquarters very confused as to what was going on. In November 1947, Humphries expressed concern about two of the Polish surveyors in a letter to Wiggins in Nairobi:

Do you know anything about the arrival of Bere's Poles? They've been gone from here now about a month and we've heard nothing. You might tell Bere to keep us more in the picture, also to let us have field books as they are completed. It is five weeks since we had his last lot and we want them urgently for this ground-nut area.[3]

Two weeks later, he wrote again:

We still have no notification from Bere that his two Poles arrived . . .
You might chase Bere about this side of his job; we so far have no report

from him for October and as a result are quite in the dark about what he is doing.[4]

It is easy to see that this period of the Directorate's life was both frustrating and exciting. Frustrating because of the constant changes of programme yet exciting because there were real users out there trying to change the prospects for whole countries. Exciting too because the Directors had such power of rapid decision making. No one seriously disputed the economic justification for mapping – many officials had seen the benefits for themselves at first hand during the War. Rapid decisions could be, and were, taken – whether it was to take up the mapping of a couple of sheets because a scientist from the International Red Locust Organisation had come into Headquarters and described the sudden onset of a new outbreak of the insects or to redeploy surveyors from one Colony to another to provide the ground control for a new development scheme.

This freedom to make decisions within the very broad control of a financial grant spread over ten years may sound strange today but it reflected the spirit of post-war Britain and the sense of trust and teamwork that had come down from the War. Hotine knew his job and knew his customers and he was allowed to get on with it. There were undoubtedly cases of irritation when a Colony's immediate needs could not be met because of commitments elsewhere which had been given higher priority. However, in general, Hotine's standing and his no-nonsense approach ensured general acceptance of his decisions. It also, of course, helped that the services he was offering came free.

Chapter 7
Early Maps

The intention during the planning stages in 1944 had been that the Directorate would adopt an orderly approach and take up large blocks of mapping in several Colonies at once. As these were completed, new blocks would be taken up in their place until complete countries were covered. In reality, of course, it was not like that at all. Firstly, it was a major challenge to base the whole mapping programme on air photography. No organisation had committed itself solely to this method before. There were no reliable guides to production times and inevitable difficulties in adapting the method to regular, routine production. Secondly, where projects were concerned, the maps were required so quickly that only those sheets specifically covering the project area were produced. This led to very irregular patterns of mapping coverage, such as the corridor along the proposed Central African Rail Link.

Early Annual Reports mention the difficulty of achieving 'maximum balanced production'. This meant having the right number of surveyors producing ground control at the right time for the photogrammetrists to scale and plot from the photography so that their plots would keep the cartographers fully occupied in fair-drawing the maps for printing. Equally important was the avoidance of undue delay in the take-up of each stage of the work after the previous stage had been completed.

It was also anticipated that the maps themselves would be comprehensive in content and contoured. Early work in the West Indies conformed to this ideal but, very quickly, it was realised that the demands coming in from throughout the Colonial Empire could not be met in reasonable time without some compromise. This led to the introduction of Preliminary Plots – simple maps showing major road and river features, the positions of the centre point of each air photograph but no contours. The 1948–9 Annual Report stated:

> Demands have poured in to the Directorate from all concerned with
> Colonial Development. The universal cry is 'Give us something now; we

46

cannot wait for the finished elaborate topographical series of maps.' Every effort has been made to meet all such demands and so called 'Preliminary Plots' have been issued in considerable numbers. The effect of production of such plots of many isolated areas upon the preparation of standard topographical series has been adverse, but worth while. [1]

In really urgent cases, where there simply were not the field survey resources available to provide ground control, some preliminary plots were produced from unscaled photography. The relation of the detail locally was near enough correct but the scale, latitude and longitude were approximate. This, too, reflected the prevailing attitude that any map was better than no map.

One of the Colonies which cried loudest for new mapping was Tanganyika but, when the Preliminary Plots appeared, there were complaints from some of the agricultural experts on the ground-nut schemes that the detail on the maps was so sparse that they could not be used. Hotine had the answer:

It is quite certain that you can get a good deal of preliminary information off these uncontoured preliminary plots together with stereoscopic examination of the photographs, and I can only recommend you in the strongest possible terms to try it, and try it with a completely open mind. I should certainly expect, from wide experience of such applications, that this would enable you to select and roughly to define certain areas as possibles, and to reject others as impossibles, without setting foot outside Dar es Salaam. The most promising possibilities could then be logged down for more detailed study, of which the production of contoured maps is of course only one aspect . . . by following these procedures, we can hope that the demands will be more nearly related to possible production resources . . . And I am quite certain that to follow this procedure will result in workable schemes being initiated much sooner than if you were to sit down and contoured maps to be produced everywhere first. [2]

Nevertheless, criticisms of the minimal content were accepted and, from 1949, full drainage patterns were included in the specification to help users to establish their position in relatively featureless bush. Contours were also provided for a few sheets where the justification was both strong and urgent.

As time went on, pressure for a less austere policy mounted and

Hotine acknowledged this in a reflective speech to the Photogrammetric Society in 1956:

> Those of us who have spent our lives in the Government service
> necessarily get a utilitarian outlook, because we almost never have enough
> men, money and equipment for more than bare essentials. Faced with the
> immense task, after Hitler's war, of rapidly expanding topographic
> mapping in the Colonies, starting with bare hands, we decided to do
> without buttons on the utility pants. Exceptionally and for good reason,
> we would produce a four-colour job with machine contours . . . but most
> production would have to go into a greater output of single-colour outline
> maps, uncontoured unless contours were essential for some particular
> urgent purpose. These outline maps would be completed later to more
> conventional standards, and meanwhile special steps were taken to
> facilitate the use of the original air photographs in conjunction with them.
>
>   There is some truth in the cliché that history repeats itself. A witness at
> the 1854 Departmental Committee on the Ordnance Survey said: 'Give
> me a faithful picture of rivers, streams and lakes, and I will fill in the
> mountains for myself.' A century later, we told the geologists on the
> Songea coalfields in Tanganyika that they could not get contoured maps
> in time; they too would have to fill in the mountains for themselves from
> the photographs. The answer was: 'O.K., but we must have *all* the
> watercourses; given them we shall know where the hills are.'
>
>   On the whole this austere policy worked, but there are now
> indications that we have got to let up. Complaints have been few from the
> professional types who mostly use the maps for economic development
> … But it is becoming all too clear that many others are unable to read any
> but the sort of maps they have been brought up on in this country. So, in
> future, more maps will appear with watercourses in blue, even though no
> water has run down many of them since the Flood and they could not
> possibly be mistaken for anything else if printed in black. Contoured
> editions, where these are likely to be a significant help to map-reading,
> will be produced more quickly, but necessarily at the expense of
> production elsewhere. We may even [colour-]fill some of the roads, if
> there are any roads.
>
>   But we are not going into the eye-wash and wall-paper market. We
> may have to bow the head to convention, but we are not going to bend
> the knee. We have got to make it clear that maps of undeveloped country,
> however detailed, will never be easy to read – there are simply not the
> roads there to take the third turning to the left out of – and in the absence

of enough landmarks, simple instrumental work will be required to keep tally of one's position. [3]

At this time, the term 'Preliminary Plot' was abandoned and, from 1956 onwards, new mapping was designed to be the First Edition of a national series, even if, to start with, it was printed in only two colours. The Directorate from the beginning stuck to the principle of using a standard scale and a standard sheet size based on the grid of latitude and longitude. This certainly helped to reduce the confusion that might have resulted from the initial urgent approach.

Map design was a problem in the early days, too. Specifications had to be devised as the work progressed and the cartographers became more familiar with the topography and content of the country. Unexpected features would suddenly be detected on the air photographs. One such was a 'sand dam' in Kenya – a dam full of sand with no surface water showing, the water being pumped up from below. Methods of depiction then had to be quickly worked out and agreed as the work proceeded. Teaching cartographers to recognise the various categories of tropical vegetation was another challenge. Advice was taken from the Royal Botanic Gardens at Kew and from the Directorate's own Forestry and Land Use Section and illustrated guides were prepared to ensure the correct interpretation of crops and natural vegetation from the air photographs.

Place names were another difficulty. The information had to come from the country concerned, either from local survey departments or from enthusiastic amateurs in the Colonial Service. One such officer in Barbados provided all the names for eighteen sheets of 1:10,000 mapping in his spare time and did it so well that his work was used as a model for others. There were always dangers in this approach, especially if the amateur mapmaker was also an amateur linguist. There are several hills in Kenya called 'Sijui', the Swahili word for 'I don't know' and one of the Nyasaland maps depicted a village called 'Bugair', a word that seems more of an irritated English expletive than a Chichewa place name.

In the early days, it was rarely possible to wait for any local name-gathering operation to be completed. Instead, names were taken from existing maps and reports though sometimes a little inspiration was necessary in choosing the correct feature. It was hoped that, over time, users would report errors and omissions and they were encouraged to send in comments with the offer of a free replacement map.

International boundaries were particularly sensitive as many had never been depicted in such accurate detail before. In the worst cases, the boundary definitions might not be sufficiently precise to allow unambiguous depiction. In other cases, the *de facto* boundary accepted by local administrators could differ from the line plotted with regard to the treaty definition. For example, one watershed boundary, drawn after careful examination of the air photographs, would have required the establishment of twenty new frontier posts at frequent intervals along a well-used road which had come to be regarded as wholly within one country. Consequently, it became the practice to show boundaries on the face of the map only when they were clearly acceptable to the responsible administrative authorities.

As the Directorate moved into its second decade, the resources available for a more planned approach to map production were beginning to become available. In 1959, a 'considerable increase in the number of maps published' was recorded in the Annual Report and the first signs of a national mapping programme could be seen in Basutoland, Bechuanaland, Cyprus, Jamaica, Kenya, several of the Leeward Islands, Malta, Northern Rhodesia, Nyasaland, Tanganyika and Uganda. There were smaller projects in several other countries, too.

In 1962, Wiggins, at a conference of the International Cartographic Association, summed it all up:

> I have tried to convey the often breathless haste with which all [our] maps have to be prepared, the continual search for methods which will give accuracy more quickly but with less and less control. In the sixteen years of the Directorate's life we have seldom found time to draw breath, to sit back or even to attend symposiums on cartographic and allied subjects; there has always been some problem needing urgent attention. Something of the order of one million square miles has been mapped at 1:50 000 but much remains to be done even at this scale . . . Speed of production is still the essence of the matter. [4]

Chapter 8

Shaping the Earth

Whilst he always believed that topographic maps should be the main product, Hotine was a respected geodesist and was determined that the Directorate would not neglect geodesy. Without a knowledge of the shape of the earth, it is impossible to project local topography accurately onto a flat mapping-surface. The work required the observation of a network of chains of triangulation covering each country and adequately connected to similar chains in adjacent countries. A central survey organisation was well suited to taking this regional approach. When, by the 1950s, the pressure for development mapping was easing, Hotine was able to start his surveyors working on several geodetic projects.

In Africa, because of the line of British influence running from the Cape through East Africa to Egypt, there was already a major piece of work in hand. A chain of triangulation, roughly following the meridian of 30° East Longitude and known colloquially as the 30th Arc, had been started at the beginning of the century and Hotine himself had observed an extension of the work through Tanganyika from Northern Rhodesia up to the Urundi border in the period 1931–3. This had been continued up to the Uganda border by the Tanganyika Survey Department in 1938. There was now strong scientific interest in extending the chain through Uganda and the Sudan to join up with the Egyptian triangulation in the north. This would provide valuable information about the degree of flattening of the earth. However, even without this connection, the 30th Arc provided an international framework on which to hang many of the East and Central African national triangulations and this is where the Directorate began work.

There is no doubt that geodetic triangulation was the most dramatic work that a Directorate surveyor was called upon to do. Each chain was a grand concept in itself. It swept across the landscape from mountain to mountain in giant strides; it required careful logistical planning and it gave the surveyor a wonderful opportunity to see the whole country and to enjoy a seemingly endless succession of breathtaking views. There were three phases: a reconnaissance to select the hills that would be used; station marking, when permanent concrete marks were built at the selected stations; and, finally, observation of the angles by theodolite, often involving a protracted occupation.

The reconnaissance period combined an intellectual challenge with the physical and aesthetic pleasures of hill climbing. Given a large tract of country which had no reliable maps, the surveyor had to identify the major hills and then select from them a network of intervisible stations 40 to 60 miles apart. Each station would need to see about five others, and narrow angles between stations had to be avoided. On the open plains of East Africa, peppered with large isolated mountains, this was no problem provided that the visibility was adequate. Cloud, haze and the local practice of burning during the dry season often hindered progress. One surveyor recalls an experience in Tanganyika when he needed a station on a flat ridge:

> I was having difficulty in selecting a site on a low cultivated ridge which would see hills 60 miles away in several directions. Visibility was not ideal and I could not be sure whether the haze or the ridge itself obscured the view of one of the hills. I had left my vehicle at an American missionary's house and he and his wife invited me to join them for lunch. After an unsuccessful morning, I explained the problem to my hosts. I was a little startled by the opening grace when we sat down to eat. 'Lord, we thank you for the presence of Mr Macdonald here with us today, remembering as we do the text "We know not when we entertain angels in our midst." ' However, there was more to come: 'Now, Lord, Mr Macdonald here is a land surveyor engaged in a reconnaissance for geodetic triangulation and, to do that, he needs a visibility of 60 miles. As you know, Lord, visibility down here is only 40 miles just now so, if you could see your way to increasing that visibility to 60 miles this afternoon, Mr Macdonald is going to be mighty grateful, Lord!' Sadly, angel or not, I didn't get the requested improvement![1]

Triangulation in the rain forests of West Africa and Borneo was another matter. Finding any hill in the jungle was never easy, even with local guides, but the real problem was deciding where the highest point of a hill feature actually was, when everything was clothed with trees 150 feet tall and visibility in any direction was restricted to a few yards. A mistake could have serious implications as major tree-felling had to take place in order to see out to the other hills of the chain. Tree-felling could last as long as three weeks and it was very frustrating if all that the felling revealed was a hilltop 100 feet higher, half a mile away, blocking a large part of the view. Harry Green had a lot of experience in West Africa and even he had problems in the Cameroonian rain forest:

> Njok Aiyah was a hill with two summits and the first, lower summit had been marked by four heavily blazed trees on the reconnaissance. I later found the higher summit and made my camp there, some 5 miles from the nearest village and 3000 feet above it, to make the observations. Seven outlying stations at distances up to 56 miles had to be observed and the very limited cloud-free periods meant that I was there for 24 days. During this time, one of the carriers who brought supplies from the village lost his way on the way back and everyone turned out to search for him, shouting and blowing horns and trumpets but to no avail. Happily, he reached the road three days later some distance to the north of the village.
>
> After three weeks, we were running short of supplies so I left the mountain for the day and drove into the nearest town returning to the roadhead at 4.30 pm. I realised that no carrier could get a load up the mountain and return before dark so I set off on my own. The three week sojourn on top had done nothing for my fitness and darkness found me still struggling up. When I detected a levelling off of the ground beneath my feet, I went from tree to tree feeling the trunks like a blind man until I eventually located the four blazes of the reconnaissance party on the lower summit. I had decided that I would play safe and spend the night in the open by the blazes when shouts and lights announced the arrival of a search party from my camp. I had told them that I would return that night and they had taken me at my word – a good example of the loyalty that grew up in a field party. [2]

Surveyors in Sabah and Sarawak avoided some of the problems of the rain forest by cutting the top off a tall tree, building a crude platform around it for the observer and placing the instrument directly on the flat trunk. Starting at 100 feet above the ground, they took to using higher and higher trees until they reached 200 feet. Their enthusiasm for the procedure was slightly diminished when a snake reared up as one of them scrambled up onto the platform. He nearly fell off with fright. The snake received an equal shock but departed more gracefully.

Angle observation was an altogether more relaxed phase of the work. At each distant station, the target for observation was, by day, a heliograph reflecting the sun's rays and, by night, a focused electric lamp. Observing sessions were timed for the early morning, mid-day, late afternoon and night. This meant that a camp had to be established on the top of the hill for the surveyor and a support party whilst teams of local employees known as light parties camped on the surrounding hills to operate the heliographs and lamps.

The hills themselves varied from small, hot, granite inselbergs beside the road in Bechuanaland to the grand mountains of Kenya with their own temperate climates, from the sweeping views of the stations in the African Rift Valley to the cramped confines of rain forest hills in West Africa and Borneo where the only view was down a narrow line cut through the trees. The most attractive locations – the high mountains of East and Central Africa – were very often the most difficult to complete because they generated so much nocturnal cloud. If everything was perfect, the observing could be finished in five or six hours and only one night need be spent on the summit. However, it never quite worked out like that. Too many things could go wrong.

First, the weather might clamp down on any of the hills involved; then the heliographs or lamps might be slightly off line or difficult to see because of poor visibility. In the early days, unfamiliarity with the demands of the work led many of the locally recruited light-parties to abandon their hills for a variety of reasons: the cold, anxiety brought on by the solitude or after encounters with big game, or local stories of spirits inhabiting particular summits. As time went on, many very experienced, competent and loyal men emerged but to begin with, young recruits were often taken on in the towns and then found themselves sitting on top of a mountain in a remote game reserve with only two companions for weeks at a time. Communication between surveyor and lightkeeper was primitive – a series of letter groups in Morse code to ask for more or less light and to indicate that the work was finished on one hill and that the lights should be moved round to the next station. It never occurred to anyone that the lightkeepers might like some codes to say that the food was finished or that they were surrounded by lions. It is not surprising that many hills were abandoned during the work to the intense irritation of the surveyor who would sit on his hill top and try and puzzle out why no light was shining. Was there just too much cloud or did it warrant a descent of his hill and a cross-country journey by lorry to find out what had happened to the light party?

When the light from Mnazi went off and did not reappear the following night, I decided to drive there to find out what was going on. I found the light party at the foot of the hill and they explained that they had come down because there was a *juju* on the hill at night. There was an hour of daylight left so I demanded that they pack up their camp and come back up the hill with me so that we could view the *juju* at first hand in the dark. We duly arrived on top at dusk and sat down to wait. Sure enough and to my complete surprise, after half an hour or so, a light began to move slowly from side to side among trees on a lower ridge half a mile away. It looked very peculiar and it took some time to realise that it was caused by the headlights of a distant vehicle on a road on the plains below which pointed straight towards the hill and meandered a little from a straight line. By a fluke, the light passed through the trees before reaching us on top of the hill. We followed the light as it came closer and eventually the lightkeepers accepted my explanation. It was only then that I gave some thought to the problem of descending the hill in the dark. In my irritation on arrival, I had omitted to bring one of my own team with me and had no torch. The lightkeepers told me cheerily that they had seen leopards on the hill. Somewhat chastened and rather scared, I set off down in the light of the stars. As it turned out, my only misadventure was to fall in an old pit designed to catch the leopards that I was now so worried about and, two hours later, I reached the safety of our camp. [3]

It was not just the inexperience of the local staff that could slow things down. Some surveyors had had little prior experience of the demanding standards of care required in the observing phase. Wiggins ended one reply to a request for advice from the field thus:

To cheer you, it should be said that first class results are often obtained from what would appear to be poor observations. Over-anxiety to obtain consistency is love's labour lost. The consensus of opinion is that 'hovering' on the target is bad alike for shooting and surveying. The best surveyors are conscientious in the erection and levelling of the instrument but quick on the draw once they are set up. [4]

Humphries took the trials and tribulations of primary observing phlegmatically. The Nyasaland chain was a particularly difficult job with many hills above 7,000 feet and a lot of cloud to contend with. Work started in March 1951 but progress was delayed by haze or by poor light-keeping when the weather was clear. The surveyors found it difficult to recruit reliable local staff who much preferred jobs in town. The vehicles were giving constant trouble and by December, when the rains set in, even Humphries was talking about a *juju* having settled on the task. As the next dry season began, he wrote to the party leader:

> You are certainly not having any luck at all with the weather so far. But it must give you a break sometime; probably it has done so already; I hope so for the sake of you and your chaps. This continuing bad weather must be sending you nigh crackers. [5]

The weather improved in the cold season but, as temperatures fell, so the rate of desertion increased. However, by July 1952, Humphries was feeling pleased:

> Your progress of observing is very cheering and it does me good to look at the Nyasaland triangulation diagram and see how your observing is going steadily north. [6]

By contrast, Chris Bere, the veteran East African party leader, always expected fast results from his surveyors:

> Surely one should expect all the lights to be on and a station to be finished on the first night, or possibly the second. Over this is disappointing, over about 4 days is exasperating, and over a week is usually calamitous as the helio parties lose interest and the batteries run down. [7]

To which the rather exasperated reply ran:

> I cannot control the weather! – I cannot blow haze away! – I cannot stop one helioboy leaving the hill from a distance of 30 miles! – I cannot stop another helioboy from closing down before I sent the good-bye signal! I gather that you never experience these troubles but they still exist – at any rate on this chain. [8]

While the logistics of the observing phase were a constant challenge, there were undoubted compensations, at least for the first few days of an occupation. Sitting on the top of a mountain 7,000 feet high, eating breakfast in the warmth of the early morning sunshine with Kilimanjaro a gleaming backdrop to the wide open spaces of the Tsavo Plains below, was something that those who experienced it will never forget. There was even something magical, if all had gone to plan, about the ring of tiny, glimmering lights coming on around the horizon as dusk fell, all pointing to the observing station, their rays passing over a sleeping countryside oblivious to what was going on. The hectic logistic exercise that had been necessary to deploy the light-parties, to recruit local porters for the ascent and to climb the mountain itself was forgotten and the surveyor could relax and get on with the work. However, this enjoyment soon palled if the weather caused delays. Some stations had to be occupied for up to six weeks before a gap in the weather allowed the work to be completed. In such cases, boredom took over and it was easy to convince oneself that the next day would see the onset of raving lunacy if the cloud did not lift.

Not every country was as well endowed with suitable mountains as East Africa. In a flat area such as Gambia, there was no alternative to carrying measurements forward by an exceedingly slow process known as precise traversing. A series of short, straight lines were cut through the bush, using open ground whenever possible and trying to avoid any dense vegetation. The angles at the turning points were measured by theodolite and the legs by 300-feet tapes suspended between tripods to clear the intervening ground. This had none of the aesthetic pleasures of triangulation on the high mountains nor the satisfaction of moving across the country in bounds of 60 miles as stations were completed. The job was carried out in unpleasant conditions of heat and humidity surrounded by a host of insects. The work was tedious but demanded care and precision. Line clearing in cultivated areas led to many cases of disputed compensation but there were some trees which it was best to avoid altogether:

> Now that the topography is such that we can produce really long traverse legs, it is even more important to get the alignment established before fully cutting the lines. There are occasionally really large trees, such as kapok or baobab, which we don't want to have to cut down and a small change in direction allows us to miss them. Apart from the labour and delay of cutting, there is often some *juju* significance or the tree can be inhabited by spirits. It isn't only large trees that can be affected; the other day we had to realign the trace because we came to quite a small tree about which our labourers were unanimous that it would be death for us all if we were to cut it. It is just as well that they have plenty of local knowledge. [9]

It was not just the trees in Gambia that were dangerous. There was the dreaded Ninka Nanka, reputedly the King of Snakes:

We have been having trouble with the Ninka Nanka recently. It is reputed to be 300 feet long and to have eyes brighter than the sun. Just being looked at by him means death within seven days. This part of the country seems to be his roosting ground and the labourers are able to recognise his roosting places. They just won't be left alone near such a place and, if a group have to stay there while we are observing, they sit in a tight circle facing inwards and go positively grey with terror.

Now that the lie of the country enables us to set out much longer traverse lines, I am using the heliographs all the time for maintaining intervisibility. This led to the most dramatic Ninka Nanka incident so far. I had a helio set up in light forest on one ridge and the labourers were cutting the line on the next ridge across a broad shallow cultivated valley. Unfortunately, half a dozen men from the nearby village were walking through the fields and one happened to look up on the line of the traverse and saw the blinding light of the helio shining out of the forest. He screamed 'Ninka Nanka' and the others looked up and saw it too. They all fled back to the village and announced that they were going to die and everyone had better stay at home as the beast was lurking just above their fields.

Later, our Gambian surveyor went to the village and found it in uproar. He tried without success to persuade them that it was not Ninka Nanka. So next day we went down with a helio and showed them what we had been doing. They eventually accepted our explanation which undoubtedly saved their lives. They really do believe in Ninka Nanka and will certainly die if the superstition says they ought to. This was a salutary lesson to us to make sure that all the local villagers know what we are doing and what equipment we are using. [10]

In 1957, the measurement of distance was transformed by a new instrument invented in South Africa which used microwaves and was virtually independent of the weather. The Tellurometer, as it was called, heralded a revolution in surveying techniques but, at first, the claims of the manufacturer for its accuracy and performance were regarded with disbelief and derision by much of the profession. Humphries, however, was impressed and resolved to carry out a trial through the flat plain of the Tana River in Kenya where, until then, slow and expensive precise traversing would have been necessary. He flew out to Kenya to supervise the trial, much to the concern of the surveyors who were not used to such close contact with Directing staff. It was a complete success. Using 60-foot towers, a total distance of 400 miles was measured in twenty-eight days. Using the old method would have taken twenty-eight months.

The Tellurometer could measure distances up to 60 miles, and sometimes more, directly and in a matter of minutes. Tape measurement and triangulation were consigned to history. At each station, only one angle had to be observed, in contrast to up to six with triangulation. The instruments had in-built telephone communication which further improved the efficiency of the operation. For the first time, each surveyor knew precisely what his colleagues were doing and there was no longer any need to rely on erratic signalling techniques. The net result was a huge saving in time and money and, once the Kenya results had been analysed and found to be of the necessary standard, traversing using Electronic Distance Measurement (EDM) became the norm for the great majority of field tasks. The Directorate, as a result of Humphries' enthusiasm, was the first major organisation in the world to adopt the new method.

Until the arrival of the Tellurometer, the lack of hills in the desert interior of Bechuanaland had precluded any form of triangulation. With the new instrument, it was possible to contemplate a series of traverses on observing towers 77 feet high criss-crossing the country. The Directorate agreed to start this work in 1962 and, as time went on, the surveyors and the locally recruited Tswana tower-builders became highly proficient in the technique. Reconnaissance was no longer necessary; traverses were run along tracks crossing the flat Kalahari Desert and the stations simply had to be 17 miles apart to allow for the curvature of the earth and the height of the trees. Once the truck milometer showed that 17 miles had been travelled, the site was selected, six large holes were dug and levelled to take the tower feet, and building commenced. Two towers were used, an inner one to take the instrument and a separate outer one for the observer. There were seven sections of 11 feet each and a human chain was used to raise the steel girders to the working level. The riggers worked in pairs, one sitting with the spanner and bolts and one standing holding the uprights in place. Safety depended on balance and nerve, the use of safety harnesses having been rejected because of the disconcerting effect of a restraining strap. It required a cool head to hold up the final upright at a height of 66 feet with no means of support other than one's knees pressing into the back of the second rigger, poised to insert the bolts.

Injuries during construction were few but the towers were not the place to be when cumulus clouds crept up during the night. The metal rails would then start to flame with St Elmo's Fire as the static electricity discharged and it was difficult in such circumstances to give due weight to the value of the instruments and the importance of preserving them. Peter Gibbs evacuated a tower one night as dark clouds approached:

> I told Sammy, the light keeper, to watch a nearby black cloud and, if it approached, to come off the tower but to leave the light shining to the other surveyor. Shortly afterwards, as I ate my supper in the tent, the storm struck with lightning and torrential rain. When the noise abated, I went out to check that the light was still shining. I could see nothing and was about to berate Sammy when my eyes grew accustomed to the dark and I realised that the tower had collapsed and fallen between my tent and those of the men 25 yards away. It had been felled by a direct strike and the equipment lay scattered on the ground. After that, we took more care to ensure that our tents were always at least 78 feet from the base of the tower![11]

The tower-builders were eventually able to dismantle a tower, move it to a new location and erect it again in a space of ten hours. With little interference from the weather, the rate of progress could be predicted with an accuracy unheard of in the days of triangulation. The satisfaction that was derived from this consistent and steady progress went some way to compensate for those tropical evenings on the mountain tops. But the days of triangulation are undoubtedly those that most surveyors remember as the peak of their experience.

Chapter 9

'And I'm Being Paid for This?'

In those early days, long-distance travel was a privilege enjoyed only by the few. When the experiences of living in the African bush were thrown in as an extra, it was not surprising that many surveyors would reflect on a day's events and feel slightly surprised that, as an additional bonus, they were being paid as well. In later years, tourists would pay to experience a similar life, in a rather contrived way on a fortnight's holiday. For the surveyor, it would last several months at a time.

The atmosphere of an overseas survey party could be quite a culture shock for new recruits. In the beginning, many travelled out by sea together with the heavy equipment. Air travel was noisy, uncomfortable and not without danger. Even Hotine baulked at crossing the North Atlantic by air in 1949 and insisted on taking a freighter from Avonmouth to Trinidad, a voyage of over two weeks, at the start of one of his directorial tours. Once arrived in the West Indies, he was quite happy to entrust himself to the airlines again. By the early 1950s, travelling by air – in first class – was beginning to be the accepted method but flights still had an atmosphere of uncertainty about them. Henry Szmuniewski, a Polish recruit, received somewhat vague instructions when travelling out to Northern Rhodesia in 1948:

> You are to proceed on flight No. BO101/6 to Lusaka, which is due to leave this country on 30th May . . . It appears likely that you will have to change aircraft at Nairobi. [There] you should, if you have time, report to Lieut. Col. G.J. Humphries at the offices of the East African High Commission in Shell House, De la Mare Avenue.
>
> On arrival at Lusaka you will find instructions to cover your onward journey. You will be working under the instructions of Mr. F.W. Sutton who may be in Lusaka when you arrive, but who is more likely to be near Chirundu. [1]

Peter Opie-Smith was a new recruit in 1953, flying out to Tanganyika with two others to join a new field party under the legendary
Chris Bere. Bere was moving up from Northern Rhodesia after
completing work on the Central African Rail Link:

> We were dressed in suits and two of us had hats and we had just flown out
> first class and stopped off at the two best hotels in Africa on the way.
> After the long train journey through the night from Dar es Salaam to
> Dodoma, we were greeted under the station lights in a cloud of flying
> insects by a surveyor immaculately dressed in torn shirt and plimsolls
> with holes in the toes. He produced a clapped out pickup truck and asked
> if one of us would mind sitting in the back for the 160 mile journey over a
> dusty, rutted road to Iringa.[2]

Bere was not one for the comforts of normal life. His base in Dar
es Salaam consisted of a number of long thatched huts built by the
military with steel mesh and mosquito gauze along the sides instead
of windows. It was an ideal base for bachelors even if it was overrun
by rats, bats and termites. The surveyors slept four or five to a room
but many were away for weeks at a time, leaving only their wooden
camp beds to mark their place. There was not enough space for
surveyors' storage so there were little piles of unwanted kit at
intervals along the corridor. The whole place was dark and gloomy
but Bere liked it that way so that surveyors spent as little time as
possible in base. When a group of six surveyors expressed surprise at
having to leave for the bush on a Sunday, he responded: 'Well, in
that case, you must go with my blessing!' Even Christmas was not
sacrosanct as Opie-Smith soon found out:

> My first Christmas, in 1953, was spent alone in a Whymper tent near the
> Rufiji delta. I had made the mistake of returning to Dar in mid December.
> I can't remember if it was a calculated decision or whether it was enforced
> by the need for more supplies but in any case I felt it was time to revisit the
> bars and bright lights of Dar with colleagues and friends from the local
> survey department. I had been in the bush for some time, on the start of
> the primary chain that was to enclose Tanganyika and eventually meet up
> with the 30th Arc near Lake Nyasa. The weather had been bad and many
> tracks were in a poor state. There were few hills in the delta and the recce
> had not gone well so I was looking forward to a break. Chris had other
> ideas and I was told to get out again as soon as possible. I said it hardly
> seemed worth the long 5-hour journey to the Rufiji and a similar journey

back at Christmas. 'Quite right!' said Chris, 'Don't bother to come back until mid-January.' Although they were mainly Muslims, I gave my men Christmas Day off, and sat in front of the tent drinking tea made with bad water and watching the ants eating the table legs. [3]

Fortunately, the excitements, the wonder and the beauty of the African bush more than made up for these privations. Much of the work was in uninhabited country at a time when big game was plentiful. One surveyor encountered more than a hundred rhino on foot in nine months; climbing a tree to avoid a charge was something most people did routinely. Elephants were a particular nuisance in camp as Gordon Meggitt recorded in his monthly diary sent to Headquarters:

Today was far from dull. While still dark I was pleased to be awakened by my cook evidently industrious in moving about the boxes under the flysheet of my tent while carrying out the early morning chores in good time. I soon dozed off, to be awoken again by a continuous glug-glug-glug noise outside my tent which was clearly a large water drum being emptied. It was still dark. Peering out into the darkness, I was not a little taken aback to see a large elephant standing 10 ft from the entrance of the tent – the only opening to a Whymper – drinking the water from the drum which he had over-turned. Bearing in mind an elephant is 14 ft long, not counting 8 ft of trunk, and 8 ft high, at 10 ft it was quite an eyeful.

It so happened that for the first time in many weeks I had left my rifle in the lorry and I was therefore unable to do anything at all. The traditional expedient of disappearing under the blankets was not, I felt, the answer. I clearly could not open the door of the tent, still less get out, without being seen. I was at a further disadvantage having just left my bed naked and quite unequipped for a prolonged sprint through uncompromising African bush. I therefore resolved to die with my boots on, and hurriedly dressed.

There was more noise. I looked out again and the elephant was in exactly the same place, but the water had ceased flowing from the drum, and he was violently rocking it with his trunk in order to get more. After a while, obviously annoyed that the water had finished, he settled to idly 'pawing' the drum with his trunk and meditating on his next course of action. Meanwhile I, with fewer possibilities to choose, was doing the same.

Allowing for the drag in time in such cases, we must have been thus transfixed for ten minutes, before he strolled round the tent and I rocketed out into space. Having cleared a large distance in a short time, I began to notice my boys in ones and twos behind bushes, all stark naked. In times of stress, they are less inhibited about such things.

The full story as I heard it then was even more startling. The beginning had evidently been when my headman had been about to use strong words on another who had rudely pushed him with a foot. He had been in the act of striking the offending foot when another boy firmly dragged him in the opposite direction. The headman, by then wide awake, realised something was wrong by the fact that the remaining porters were rapidly and silently crawling out of the tent. The elephant, whose trunk was the foot, continued to feel about in the tent and then gently shook the tent pole without knocking it down. It then turned to rocking the lorry with the driver unable to move because of his thorough tying of the tarpaulin with him inside. Its next move was to knock my food boxes about and waken me.

By 5.30, all the boys were collected together and the elephant had retired. At 6.00, the elephant reappeared, quickly scattered everyone from the camp again by a gentle feint and charge and then once more began knocking about the water drums. It was 8.00 before he moved sufficiently for us to reoccupy the camp. Not feeling very hungry we left immediately for work. Returned for breakfast at 3.00pm. [4]

Of all the remote areas in which the Directorate had to work, the Selous Game Sanctuary in Tanganyika was perhaps the most demanding. There were virtually no roads and most hills involved a long march with at least one night on the way. The surveyor's instruction for reaching Mkunghu hill was fairly simple: 'Walk for 40 miles from Kiberege on a bearing of 100°.' The journey took three days and the surveyor added the laconic comment: 'much big game'. Robin Auld was one of the surveyors who worked there:

Within ten minutes of leaving the hill, we were charged by an old bull buffalo, which the Game Guard despatched with efficiency. In an endeavour to find more water, we made for a river valley and after a nine hour walk, came to the village of Kilengwe. En route, we had a real fright from a group of five elephants, including a mother and baby. The whole safari must have passed within 20 yards of them. The bush was extremely thick but, just as we emerged into the open river bed, there was a terrifying trumpeting close by. The porters dropped their loads and

17 The old and the new – the last crossing of the Mungo River in the Southern Cameroons by dugout canoe in 1959. *A S Macdonald*

18 Surveyors' longboat negotiating the easier section of the Talong Rapids, Sarawak, 1971. Expensive surveying equipment was always unloaded for these passages! *J Laughton*

19 Hitching a lift from a local mine train in the rainforest of Guyana in the 1980s. *Crown copyright*

20 George Reid (surveyor, left), Frank Smith and Norman Parrin about to set off with horses to climb Mt Moody in the Falkland Islands in the winter of 1959. Blizzard conditions were frequent at the summit camp and Reid had to stay for three weeks before the work could be completed. *J M Evans*

21 Pacific idyll – unloading from MV *Kangava*, anchored off Malaita, British Solomon Islands, 1964. *P Opie-Smith*

22 The beach in Sarawak was one of the few open spaces in the country and traverses were run along the coast using DIY towers to allow greater distance between stations. Here, W R Cooper, of the Department of Land and Surveys, is observing while A S Macdonald and other employees help to unload the boat. In the background, a Melanau fisherman departs for quieter waters. Annual Report, 1961. *Crown copyright*

23 The morning after – Hendrik, Devson and Johannes survey the wreckage of a 77-foot observing tower felled by a nocturnal thunderstorm in Bechuanaland in 1965. *P McC Gibbs*

24 Peter King taking angle observations with a theodolite on the beach at Betio, Gilbert and Ellice Islands, 1970. *Crown copyright*

25 In the flat lands in the west of Northern Rhodesia in 1962, the surveyors built these elevated observing platforms to increase the distance that could be measured between stations. For obvious reasons, they were called 'Alamos'. Edwin Furmston observing. *P McC Gibbs*

26 Robert Chagoma, the Chief Headman in Bechuanaland from 1962 until his death in 1980. He joined the Directorate in 1949 in Nyasaland, also served in Northern Rhodesia and earned the greatest respect from all the many surveyors with whom he worked. *P McC Gibbs*

27 John Evans using the Tellurometer under winter conditions at Mt Round in the Falkland Islands in 1959. Nowhere else did surveyors have to put up with such cold weather. *C G Brading*

28 George Godon, one of the original Polish recruits, identifies his location on the aerial photographs (using the termite mound which will be clearly visible) while John Issa reads the altimeter – Tanganyika, 1960. *Crown copyright*

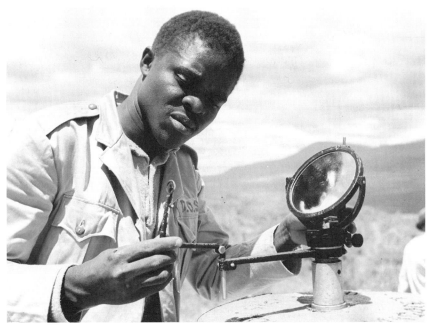

29 Joseph Okoth, a lightkeeper with the Kenya party, lines up his helio on a distant hill, preparatory to shining a light to the surveyor there. *Crown copyright*

30 A palm tree is used to support a DIY tower construction during a survey of Kambia township. Sierra Leone, 1968. *R Wood*

31 Early morning at 16,000 feet on Mt Kenya, waiting for the cloud to clear and allow observations to start, 1954. *Crown copyright*

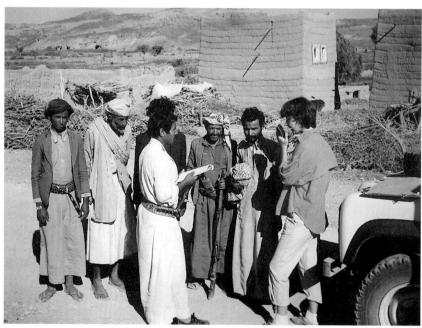

32 Julia Cogan and her Yemeni assistant record the name of a village from local inhabitants in the Yemen Arab Republic in the 1980s. Great care was taken to obtain the correct name which was recorded in both spoken and written form. *Crown copyright*

scattered and, as there were 50 of them, I had to take a roll call afterwards to make sure everyone was safe. [5]

A few days later, he was again in trouble:

The following morning I broke camp at the hippo pool. The loads were just about to be issued to the porters when I had the misfortune to be stung on the neck by a scorpion which had secreted itself in my beret. A rapid perusal of the Fitzsimons' snake-bite pamphlet did nothing to inspire confidence, as it only mentioned the rather ghastly symptoms but offered no remedy. I had the sting cut out and rubbed in permanganate. Kilengwe was only five hours walk so I walked there, putting myself at only a few hours' walk from the truck in case matters became worse. However, though feeling rather tired and suffering from a severe headache for 48 hours, I was able to return to the waterhole the following day. [6]

Further north, in the Tsavo National Park in Kenya, George Godon, one of the Polish surveyors, was reporting his experiences to Humphries:

North of Galana River I was forced to long walks and to cross the river on foot many times. Crocodiles in my vicinity were a source of danger. Along the escarpment north of Galana, the work was disturbed on many occasions by rhinos. I was charged many times by them, and once one of my labourers was knocked down receiving only slight scratches and nervous shock. This accident happen [sic] only few yards from me and good luck was with me. We started to walk in this area very carefully and slowly, but climbing trees on many occasions. From my recent experience, no weapon or askari can help as rhinos hidden in thick bush are charging from very short distances . . . I am very pleased working in this area which is interesting and quite wild. [7]

There were ways of protecting yourself from such encounters as Don Cregeen discovered:

We camped on top of a hill in the Selous Sanctuary and there was a large herd of elephants on the plain below. One evening the whole herd came wandering across the hill near the camp. We were all getting just a bit anxious when one of my men said that he had an elephant *juju* and would tell the elephants not to come any nearer. He walked down right into the middle of the herd, although it contained many mothers with calves. When he came back, he said that the elephants had agreed to stay away and they certainly never came near again. [8]

It was an energetic life: Roy Wood kept a record of his climbs during his tours and, in one six-month period in 1953, he walked 675 miles, climbed 44 mountains (defined as requiring a climb of 1,000 feet or more) and 62 hills. The following year, on a 25-day safari, he covered 237 miles and climbed 5 mountains and 11 hills. [9] The energetic, sometimes exhausting days made the evening a particularly enjoyable time. Clean and cool, one could sit back and soak up some of the sights and sounds of the country. The sun might be setting in a riot of colour against a background of distant hills or dipping into the evening calm of the ocean. From a mountain top, as the colours of the sunset dimmed, the fires in distant villages could be seen and the sounds of village life could be clearly heard in the still air. In the game parks, the lions started their endless conversations and were joined by a whole orchestra of other animals more difficult to identify. By the beach, the calmer seas of the night slop-slopped onto the sand and a cool breeze sighed through the casuarina trees. Whatever was in store for the morrow, the present seemed perfect, the job a privilege and the rat race in Britain a million miles away.

Chapter 10
Co-Workers and Companions

If the surveyors had to work hard, their local employees had to work much harder in terms of physical effort. Carrying loads up hills or on long safaris was acceptable from time to time but, when it went on for two or three weeks without a break, they began to complain. There was no reason why they should share the impatience of the surveyor to get on with things. Throughout the life of the Directorate, surveyors became surprisingly angry and irritated at anything that caused delay or interference with the smooth running of their work. Administrators, garage mechanics, ferrymen, wives and local staff – all from time to time incurred their wrath and, of course, in the days when Colonial attitudes still prevailed, the local staff often saw more of their wrath than the others.

Surveyors behaved towards their employees according to the mores of the time. In the early days, this meant that some fairly rough justice was handed out. Porters who refused to carry a load, or who deserted risked being reported to the local chief who might well decide to flog them. In difficult areas, a policeman might accompany the foot safari to maintain discipline. Hotine was described as a true Christian gentleman by one of his staff at Headquarters and he gave an interesting insight into his views on race when giving the inaugural lecture to the Land Surveyors' Division of the Royal Institution of Chartered Surveyors in 1949. Once again, he seems to have been well ahead of his time:

Racial co-operation is particularly important in the Colonies and will rapidly become even more so . . . Treat members of other races just exactly as you would treat Englishmen in a comparable way of life. And if you are deterred solely by fear of the consequences from going around kicking *English* agricultural labourers in the place which you believe Nature intended for that purpose, then stay out of the Colonies. You will be no use there, or anywhere else for that matter, in a position of some authority. Avoid like the plague using or even thinking the word

'Native', particularly in the hearing of the educated who may well know more about the English language than you do. [It] conveys a suggestion of 'airy nothing', the sole quality of having been born somewhere. The word 'African' for example covers a multitude of skins, and pride of race, from Arab, Boer and Copt to Yoruba and Zulu; but it does at any rate allow a man a 'local habitation and a name', if only a Continent. [1]

Young men were recruited in town and expected to carry heavy loads up large mountains or for long distances across country. One headman in Nyasaland would recount how, when first employed, he had been sent on foot to carry a message from a surveyor on one hill to a colleague on another. He descended a 6,000-foot escarpment, walked 25 miles, climbed a 3,000-foot hill and delivered the message. Next day, he returned with the reply. When he staggered to the top of the escarpment, all he had to show for his exertions was the simple message: 'Yes'.

Many of the camps were at altitudes that the men were not used to and a single blanket was often the only acknowledgement of their need for protection from the cold. If they were members of a light-party, it would be a lonely and self-reliant life, far from habitation in a strange part of the country and subject to the worrying and unfamiliar sounds of the bush at night. Mountains were often associated with spirits, a belief that the impatient surveyor dismissed out of hand but one that had very real power for the young recruit.

Encounters with wild game were frequent and, in one case in 1950, fatal:

> Due to shortage of labour, we used only to take a blanket and a ground sheet for sleeping on. Lying there at night, one could hear the lions roaring around and the hyenas giving vent to their peculiar cry, and it was a comfort to feel the cold barrel of the gun beside you on the blanket . . . where there are hyena there are usually lion but lion are not always so obliging in warning you of their approach. This lesson was brought home to me viciously when my camp was swiftly and silently attacked by a lion, and a terrified boy carried off to be eaten. Unfortunately, at that time, I had no gun, so all that remained to be done was to spend the rest of that dreadful night up a tree. [2]

This incident did, in fact, lead to rifles being issued to all surveyors working in game country and there were fortunately no more fatal accidents of this nature.

Considered in retrospect, it is not surprising that many local employees deserted in the early days or that the field party leader in Uganda was moved to exclaim in a report to Humphries that the city boys from Kampala were quite useless. Many city boys from Birmingham would have been equally useless on a similar job in the Scottish Highlands. However, there were, of course, exceptions and Samson, a lightkeeper in Northern Rhodesia was one, as Richard Bardua recalls:

> I was working on a chain along the Northern Rhodesia – Belgian Congo border when a distant light went out one night just before I had finished. I decided to move on to the hill in question which was my next observing station. We crossed the border into the Congo and took a small bush track to the foot of the hill. Usually, the light-party, on hearing the lorry, would come down the hill to greet us but not on this occasion. Our camping kit was unloaded and carried up the hill and, when we reached the top, we found Samson, the lightkeeper and one of the labourers building an impressive thorn boma. They were clearly very relieved to see us: 'Bwana, we have much trouble! We think we will die! Last night, lions come. Aloo and I climbed a tree. Greenwell ran away and hasn't come back.'
>
> The previous evening, when they started to shine their lamp to my hill, they could hear lions roaring in the distance, too far away to cause concern. Around midnight, the two of them were sitting by the pillar waiting for my signal to finish work when suddenly a lion roared close by. They both leapt up, knocking the lamp off line in the process, and climbed a tree. From the branches, they watched first one lion and then a second walk up to the pillar, sniff around and then lie down beside it. Greenwell, who had been in the tent, had made a rapid exit and could be heard crashing through bushes on his way down the hill but the lions took no notice of him.
>
> Samson and Aloo spent the night up the tree tied to its branches with their belts in case they fell out on top of the lions. They must have dozed off and, when they woke, it was light and the lions had disappeared. They climbed down cautiously and explored the area around. There were no signs of the lions – or of Greenwell. So they set to and started building a thorn boma to protect themselves on the following night, which, in the circumstances, was a fairly courageous course of action![3]

After an eventful couple of nights' work, frequently interrupted by the approach of the lions, Bardua returned to his base camp in

Northern Rhodesia where Greenwell arrived a day or two later having walked all the way through the bush.

His experiences on the journey went unrecorded but foot safaris in game country could be a stressful experience for porters who had not been far from their villages before:

> 16th: Move north having to leave much behind, including all tents, radio, some food and beacon building materials. Porters very slow. Make camp by River Apon. Porters agitated by elephant.
>
> 17th: Go north east across the Apon. Recce in the north east corner of heighting area. Delayed by wart hog, buffalo and on the return in the evening by elephant for some time. They finally stampeded from fire. Reached camp at dusk.
>
> 18th: Moved camp up to the watershed. The porters who came behind dropped their loads in an incident with elephant. No damage.
>
> 20th: Recce along watershed. Observing delayed and disturbed by buffalo. All camp out to buffalo at night.
>
> 21st: Rain in the middle of the day. At night all camp fled in confusion when an elephant equally startled walked in and bellowed frightfully. A few minor cuts and bruises, no serious damage but porters more insistent about 'wanting to go home'.
>
> 22nd: More observations until disturbed and forced to move away by elephant also a rhino but this moved on without interference. Recce down the watershed with camp 6 miles. Heavy rain at night.
>
> 24th: Recce 6 miles SW and heighting. Met lion on way out and driving rain all the way back. Camp had to be left because of elephant during my absence. Lion around again at night, but we were not disturbed. [4]

However, in every labour force there were those who actually enjoyed the life and, with time, these reached sufficient numbers to provide a core of reliable, confident workers who would stick to the job in spite of severe provocation. As Kozlowski reported in 1960: 'Mr Godon found his base altimeter reading party sitting in the top of a tree with the elephants under the tree in the shade of it. Fortunately, they had taken their altimeter with them so no work was lost.' [5]

All local employees were on temporary terms because of uncertainty about the length of their employment. As it turned out, in several countries, the work went on for thirty years or more and, as the years went by, they acquired wide experience of each country and its hills. Though they strenuously denied it at every opportunity, they appeared to enjoy the physical challenge of the work, the camaraderie of the camp fire and the constant movement. In older parties, the Chief Headmen became, over time, figures of immense stature. Samuel Mbathi in Kenya, Beaton Njanji in Malawi, Estin Nkwaila in Zambia, Robert Chagoma in Bechuanaland and Henry Matthew and Peter St Joseph in the West Indies were just a few of those who are remembered with affection and respect by all those surveyors who worked with them. They were dedicated employees – Njanji even named one of his children after Wiggins when a son was born during the night of the Director's visit to the field party; the Director himself seemed a little nonplussed by the honour. Nothing daunted, Njanji named his ninth child, born in 1977, after the author. Njanji, Nkwaila and Chagoma all came from Malawi; there seemed to be a particular rapport between surveyors and Malawians. They enjoyed travel and the Directorate's lifestyle suited them well. Before independence, many of them worked for the Directorate in Northern Rhodesia, Bechuanaland and Basutoland as well as in their own country. Chagoma sadly died of a heart attack in Bechuanaland. Once again, the Directorate's ability to show compassion when it was needed came to the fore. Although there was no precedent, his body was flown back to Malawi so that his family could arrange and attend the funeral. When the Zambia party closed down in 1980, an appeal to surveyors who had worked in the party over the previous twenty years raised some £300 for a farewell party for the men and their families. In 1984, when the Malawi party closed down, an even larger sum was raised in similar fashion. All these events were well-earned tributes to the contribution that these men had made and to the companionship that they had provided on so many hard days in the bush.

Chapter 11

Safaris, Ulendos and Treks

Whether you were on safari in East Africa, on *ulendo* in Central Africa or trekking in Basutoland, one fundamental requirement of the field work was to move about the country as quickly and as reliably as possible. Maintaining various forms of motorised transport in working order under harsh conditions was to become one of the biggest sources of stress in a surveyor's life. However, the Directorate started life at a time when motor transport was still a novelty to many and this might explain the initial reluctance of the Directing staff to provide surveyors with any transport at all.

There would have been anxieties about providing such transport on two counts. It was seen both as a luxury and as a source of uncontrollable expenditure on fuel, repairs and maintenance. Furthermore, Wiggins and Humphries, from their pre-war experience in Nigeria, would have considered it unlikely that vehicles would be of much use in a lot of the terrain in which the teams would be working and where motorable tracks would be few and far between. The most economical procedure would therefore be to hire or borrow vehicles from local Government sources to get the surveyors into an area, after which they would walk to work from a central camp.

This reliance on local support did not work well in practice. The first field party in the Gold Coast quickly found that the local Survey Department had its own commitments which took priority. Transport was extremely difficult to procure at short notice and on specific days. Within two weeks of his arrival, Walter Smith was writing home on Boxing Day, 1946:

> Transport is a headache and no one here seems remotely interested in helping me to get any from the local department. Is it possible, please, for something to be done before it is too late? At the moment, I am forced to plan a considerable waste of public money and time through sending surveyors off [on foot] along a stretch of fifty miles of motorable road to tie in to an existing beacon every two or three miles. People here say that

they did all their [survey work] on foot . . . maybe, but it wasn't air
survey, an economical method of 1946 . . . I want to do this job of
ground survey by methods as economical as the air survey which is going
on overhead. [1]

And two days later, in a hurried note in pencil:

. . . the D.C. told me that he did not expect the party to stay in the field
much longer unless they got a jeep or light vehicle to ferry water and food
to them. Apparently their next stretch is a forty mile one without water –
all that I can get is one water container and a few buckets . . . I'm doing
my level best to hire a jeep in Accra but it's quite hopeless. [2]

However, after a further two days of chasing in Accra, Smith took
the decision to buy a second-hand jeep on his own authority. A week
later, Wiggins cabled the Governor requesting his help in the
purchase of a lorry and Smith had the transport that he needed.

Even in East Africa, with its much larger road network, Chris
Bere was given no transport when he first arrived. Eventually he was
allowed one pickup to share between four surveyors. Some surveyors resorted to flagging down the infrequent trains for a lift.
Gradually, the need for transport was accepted but it was never easy
to get and there were still complaints of delays caused by having to
share vehicles.

Travelling by lorry was not a comfortable experience in the early
days:

There were virtually no surfaced roads, except a few in the larger towns.
Travelling on dirt roads was a pain, the lorry trailing a swirling, choking
plume of red dust. You rattled over potholed and corrugated earth tracks
that loosened your teeth in their sockets. Mechanical problems and
punctures inevitably caused delays. At one time, I averaged one broken
spring a month on my lorry. And radiators were forever springing leaks
due to vibration. Fortunately, a handful of maize meal in the water helped
as a temporary seal, an African style Holt's Radweld.

Rivers, even dry ones, could pose difficulties. Bridges often consisted
of Y-shaped tree trunks set in the bed of the river with other tree trunks in
the Y's, spanning across the stream bed. The deck was then made up of
transverse planking. Some of the structures were extremely rickety and
inspection was advisable before crossing. On one occasion I was so
concerned that I unloaded the truck and, showing my cowardly streak,

told driver Mohammed to drive the empty lorry over while I 'supervised' from the far side. Happily only one wheel went through the deck and Mohammed's panic-stricken burst on the accelerator got the lorry across. A few bridges were decked transversely with bamboo, lashed together rather like a mat. These were horrendous to watch. As the lorry crossed the bridge, the bamboo 'mat' lifted in a sort of wave, travelling in front of the lorry wheels.

Drifts could be difficult too. If paved with a narrow raised concrete causeway and with water flowing over, it was impossible to see exactly where the causeway was. One had to fix one's eye on the far bank and endeavour to cross in an exact straight line. Failure to do so could result in dropping a wheel over the edge of the causeway. Unpaved drifts always held the possibility of getting stuck in the deep sandy river bed but this was a relatively minor problem, unless rain had fallen in the hills and a flash flood came down. [3]

It might have been uncomfortable for those in the cab but the unfortunates who had to travel in the back had an even worse time:

Up to six labourers were required to lie horizontally in the narrow space between the roof and the pile of water and fuel drums, tents and spare springs, food sacks and boxes, paraffin and spare tyres. Once they were squeezed in, the door was closed and locked and they then endured several hours of slow, dusty travel over pot-holed and corrugated dirt tracks, emerging at the end of it more like Red Indians than African tribesmen. Those in front fared little better as the fine dust permeated everything. [4]

Ferries over large permanent rivers always incurred delay. Many were very primitive: large empty petrol drums or two dugout canoes with a plank deck and ramps either end. They were often hauled across the river by rope and human labour. The ferries over the Gambia River were always unpredictable:

We had ordered the ferry for 12.30 pm and paid for a special journey but the wretched thing was broken down at the other side. It was after 2 pm when they managed to start the engine and cross the river, which is about a mile wide. They have a little lunatic boy as one of the crew and they are always very nice to him and let him steer and work the winch which drops the bow ramp so you can imagine the chaos that can ensue. Sure enough, the boy was steering and couldn't beach the thing straight, so we had an awful job getting the vehicles on. Then, before we could start piling the rest of the kit on the deck, the ferry was rushed by hoards of locals with bicycles, handcarts and piles of luggage. The skipper said he couldn't keep them off and the local policeman said he couldn't either, even if we had paid for a special journey, as it was a public ferry. The result was that we found ourselves with the vehicles on the south bank and most of the kit on the north bank and had to send the ferry back for a second journey. It was 5 pm before the second load of kit was on the south side of the river and this time the boy ran the ferry so hard ashore that they couldn't get it off until high tide the following morning. I was still on the north bank with the last load of kit and it soon became obvious that the ferry was not coming back for us. I had no desire to spend the night at Balingho and managed to negotiate a trip across the river with a local who had a sufficiently river-worthy canoe. That canoe journey was a terrifying end to an appalling day. The current runs fast on the ebb tide and, although the river looks calm from the bank, once out in the middle in a small canoe it became very choppy. Fortunately, my ferryman was obviously used to doing the crossing and we eventually made the south bank just as it was getting dark. [5]

Early vehicles were unreliable and the rough roads inflicted harsh treatment as Richard Bardua's diary recorded in Bechuanaland in 1958:

> 5th: Set off from Maun with two trucks, one carrying 350 galls of water. Proceeded for 50 miles and waited for second truck to catch up. After 1 hour, turned back to find it broken down with stripped gears 8 miles from Maun. The driver had got a lift in and brought the LandRover out to try to tow the truck back. Result: stripped crown wheel and pinion in the LandRover! Returned to Maun. [6]

Leaving the vehicles in Maun for repair, he went back to the bush in the remaining lorry but, at the end of this trip, about 100 miles from home, the steering jammed and the truck shot off the road into the bush. He had to wait until 6 pm the next day before he could get a lift into Maun where he removed the steering controls from his garage-bound truck. It took another two days to return to the truck, change the steering units and return to Maun.

The following month, he was having more problems:

> 15th: As BPX324 had had new gear box fitted and was supposedly roadworthy, I left 325 to have springs fitted and set off to Kuki in 324.

Trouble started soon after leaving Maun: broken main leaf on rear spring,
broken exhaust pipe. Only 80 miles from Maun but had to camp and fix
spring and pipe with bits of wire, tins and what have you.
16th: Managed to cover 15 miles and the gears jammed. Opened the gear
box, put the gear in neutral but, as soon as we started moving, the gears
jammed again. Camping on the spot. [7]

On this occasion, two days passed before he got a lift and was able to
bring a mechanic back to effect a temporary repair. Two months
later, he had more trouble while working in the west of the country,
an area settled by Afrikaner farmers:

25/26th: Moved to Ghanzi. Set off to Van Zyl's farm. Truck broke down
30 miles from Dakar. Suspect crown wheel in differential. Leaving truck
behind, set off with one man to walk to Dakar, reaching it in the evening.
Got hold of Craill, the local mechanic and went back with tractor to tow
truck in. Back in Dakar 4 am.
27th: Absolutely no road traffic in Dakar, no lifts. Examined truck –
broken crown wheel and pinion – no spares available. Craill flew me to
Ghanzi camp (25 miles) but D.C. and Police officer both away. Sent radio
message to Maun for spares. Answer: mechanic is away! Return to Dakar.
Identifications at Dakar and at Berger's farm on horseback (borrowed
from local farmer). [8]

Not many surveyors could claim to have travelled by plane and on
horseback in one day! It took another two days for Bardua to get
back to Maun and two weeks to get the truck repaired.

The first surveyors into Basutoland were spared the vagaries of
the internal combustion engine. They travelled on horseback, using
mules to carry their equipment. The treks usually lasted three to four
weeks. The logistics of moving at up to 11,000 feet in the high
mountains, where there was no grazing, were complex and the
mules were constantly ferrying fodder up to the high camps. This
continuous work tended to produce back sores and the surveyors had
often to kick their heels during precious spells of fine weather
because the animals were not fit. Edwin Furmston recounted his
problems in his monthly diary:

Moved back to Ongeluk's Nek to face the rather dismal prospect of a
week waiting to try and give these sores a chance to heal – not least
because the District Commissioner in Qacha's is a pundit on animals and

I'm a bit scared in case he decides they aren't fit for work in January if he sees them around camp. 2 mules fit, 4 with healing sores and Bija with a septic gall. All the horses have one or more shoes missing and four are developing sore spots. [9]

When he was ready to move again, further trouble struck:

16th: Horses missing. Spent day scouring hills for them with no luck. They must have been stolen, I'm afraid, which will indeed be catastrophic. Somewhat of a panic day.
17th: Sent message to nearest police. Then horses turned up in distance. Examination reveals whip marks. I am convinced they must have been stolen and driven off. The culprit then found the Government branding and drove them back near enough to find their way in. Great relief. [10]

Transport breakdowns were always a source of irritation but, occasionally, the inconvenience and delay that they caused were avoided by some stroke of luck, as Paul Newby found in St Lucia:

We had left our LandRover parked under a tree beside one of those narrow, bumpy roads that lead nowhere, winding down the jungly spurs truncated by the precipitous west coast. When we got back, and tried to drive away, the engine roared but we stayed still. Puzzled, we peered underneath the vehicle. The barely credible truth was that the rear propeller shaft had disappeared.

What next? Drive off in front wheel drive and complain to the Police? Accept the fortunes of war and just order a new one from England? Set fire to the surrounding bush and see if we could flush out the thief? Some ancient memory must have stirred in one of my labourers. He suggested that we followed the track to its end.

Down through the trees we went until we reached a small clearing above the cliffs. There we found an unusually charming squatter's house. Its most striking feature was its decoration: house, garden and outhouse were encrusted with motor parts, most of them recognisable LandRover parts from the last 30 years and in apparently usable condition.

With considerable trepidation – this was clearly the home of a lunatic with a large spanner – I knocked on the front door. After a long delay, a very ancient lady appeared. I explained that we had come to collect our propeller shaft. 'Help yourself!' she said. We helped ourselves to the most likely looking example, grabbed a handful of nuts from a convenient bench and departed smartly in our vehicle before the kleptomanic husband put in an appearance. [11]

These continuing dramas over transport in the field had little effect on Treasury accountants. They were more concerned over the proper allocation of expenditure and they brought Bere to task after his first few months in Tanganyika. He was not to lump the cost of all labourers under the 'Labour' sub-head in his accounts. Those labourers used for carrying loads on foot safaris were to be charged to the 'Transport' sub-head. Even in the cavalier Directorate, the accountants could have the last word!

Chapter 12

No Place for Wives

From the start, it was seen as essential that surveyors should be mobile and prepared to move at short notice. Even when posted to a Colony, the surveyor could not be sure of spending his whole tour there. Jobs like the Central African Rail Link had shown the need to move long distances during a tour. It was therefore inevitable that Hotine should insist on unaccompanied tours of duty. He made his views quite clear to the Conference of Commonwealth Survey Officers in 1947:

> We have got to accept the fact that the average age for marriage is now less than it was; that many applicants are already married and reckon that they have had their share of separation during the war; and that the Colonial Survey Service inevitably implies some separation sooner or later. There is nothing that we can do about it. Anyone who cannot face such periods of separation had better get a job which enables him to catch the 5.30 train home every evening and face the disadvantages of that instead. The only advice I will offer the intending applicant – and I don't expect him to listen to it – is that a happy marriage cannot be founded on dead flat monotony or on selling either party 'down the river' into uncongenial employment amounting to slavery. It has been said that successful marriages result only when the contracting parties are so poor as to depend on each other for the necessities of existence or are rich enough to live apart. If that is so, the surveyor is peculiarly well placed to make a success of marriage without the disadvantages of extreme poverty or extreme riches. [1]

The Directors held the strong belief that the surveyor's job was to work in the bush for as much of the time as could be managed – the presence of a wife somewhere in the colony would only serve to distract him from that aim. Hotine himself had left his wife at home in his younger days in Africa and he had, of course, endured periods of separation during the War. He saw nothing wrong with this but, as time went on, married surveyors became more and more dissatisfied. Some, like John Alexander, ignored the rule. He brought his wife out to Kenya in 1949 at his own expense and then asked for the situation to be formally recognised. This caused Hotine to write to Humphries in Nairobi:

> I have told [Alexander] that the rule cannot be relaxed for reasons which you will appreciate and that for his wife to live in nearby farms etc. would have to be considered a plain evasion of the rules since in most cases it would result in the surveyor taking into consideration other factors affecting his moves than the run of the work.
>
>   . . . on completion of the Voi survey he will definitely have to make other arrangements to leave his wife in some definite centre or to return her to England if he wishes to remain in the employment of the Directorate. [2]

In fact, Alexander's wife continued to move about with him and, when he was sent south to work on the Rail Link, they looked for accommodation for her in Mbeya without success. In March 1951, Alexander wrote despairingly to Hotine:

> Since coming to Mbeya, my wife and I have been trying to find somewhere suitable to live for her; the hotel here is not suitable, and would also be a great drain on my resources, which I must now guard, against paying her return to England. Also your rule causes so much distress, especially to my wife, who is particularly sensitive to this measure separating us, that I must now inform you that I have her with me in camp until our return to Nairobi.
>
>   I realise that this is a statement of my resignation, and I make it very sadly, since I have been proud of working for the Directorate, and I see a marvellous future for it. [3]

Walter Smith, who had been moved from Nyasaland to work on the Rail Link in southern Tanganyika, also wished to have his wife out for a short spell but wrote first to Hotine for permission, stressing that he strongly supported the Director's view that wives had no place travelling in the bush. Hotine was unyielding in his reply:

> I am glad that at any rate we agree that surveyors' wives should not go into the bush with them or accompany them on safari. But I am sorry that we are unable to agree that that is or should be the normal life for our

surveyors while they are in the field. In my view, even when you are on minor control [work], you should move camp as often as possible in order to get right on the job as soon after first light as possible, and you should continually consider whether there is any advantage at all to be gained by moving camp – if necessary, every day . . . whatever you think about it now, I feel sure that if you had a wife there you could not avoid gravitating towards a semi-permanent base camp. [4]

Though unyielding in principle, he encouraged Smith to make any concrete suggestions which might ameliorate the situation and Smith took up the invitation, advocating that tours of duty at Headquarters should be interspersed with overseas postings and that wives should be allowed out for a limited period every third tour. He stressed that his disagreement with Hotine was not over the principle of separation but over whether it should be total and 'without end'. Hotine replied at length in a friendly but unchanged manner. Tours at home were a possibility though he thought few would find them financially attractive. Occasional visits by wives would not be supported by the Treasury who had very clear rules about the length of tours for accompanied officers and their wives in the Colonial Service in general. More positively, he said that he was trying to shorten overseas tours to nine months and even, perhaps, to increase the amount of leave if surveyors accepted seven-day working in the field. He then turned to Smith's concern that the separation was without end:

I seriously quarrel with this conclusion and indeed with such a philosophy of life altogether. There is simply no way in which anyone can foresee the whole course of his life, and if he were able to do so it would simply not be worth living. [5]

He went on to point out that Smith's chances of promotion were good and should see him out of the bush in ten to fifteen years:

Meanwhile, you may well find that conditions of existence are not ideal, but I do suggest that you do not make the mistake of supposing that there are such things as ideal conditions of existence anywhere or in any occupation. Once you and your wife get into the habit of picking bits out of other people's lives in order to make up for yourselves what you consider to be an ideal, you will forfeit all happiness in this life for ever. It is fatally easy to slide into the habit of permanent dissatisfaction and to acquire an ingrained sense of self-pity which is the most corrosive of all human diseases. The truest words ever written in the English language on this subject were by Shakespeare – 'there is nothing either good or bad but thinking makes it so'. [6]

Smith was unconvinced by his philosophical Director and resigned three months later. Others, however, chose to gamble on being too far from home for anyone to check up on them. The cost and red tape associated with travel at that time might enable Headquarters to keep a check on wives in Britain but Hotine could do little about romances that started in the colony where a surveyor was working. At the same time as Smith was receiving his long letters from the Director, other surveyors were marrying locally and taking their wives to bush.

Hotine's views were theoretically correct. Surveyors with wives living locally might well not go to bush for quite as long as bachelors but the question was really whether his policy was reasonable and sustainable. It was certainly having disastrous effects on retaining experienced surveyors. More and more voted with their feet and, in 1956, the policy was abandoned and wives were allowed to accompany their husbands abroad on alternate tours.

Chapter 13

A Broader View

By 1951, the Directorate had outgrown the huts at Bushy Park and it moved to newly built accommodation just off the Kingston by-pass at Tolworth in June. The new building was of that design that spawned a whole rash of 'Government Buildings' from Bristol to Longbenton and from Southampton to Glasgow. It was alleged that the design was originally intended for a series of emergency field hospitals during the War and continued in use thereafter because of the savings in architects' and quantity surveyors' fees. Whatever the reason, it was a boringly functional design of single-storey rectangular blocks off a central spinal corridor. There seemed to be no limit to the length of these corridors in 'Government Buildings' and the one at Tolworth was almost 300 yards long and followed the curve of the rising ground in such a way that floor level at one end was not visible from eye level at the other. Its slope meant that it was a constant experimental laboratory for non-slip surfaces. It is alleged that one Polish cartographer managed to ride a motor-cycle from one end to the other undetected. More prosaically, its length provided the facility for a wonderfully exciting display of the Directorate's products along the walls. Maps of Gambia and the Gold Coast, Dominica and Basutoland, Antarctica and Zanzibar soon graced its walls and gave an impression of clear purpose to staff and visitors alike.

The new accommodation gave adequate space to all the existing departments for the first time. Larger, more stable wooden floors for Slotted Template Assemblies were constructed, uninterrupted by any supporting pillars. The largest was 78 feet by 32 feet and allowed the assembly of blocks of templates covering areas as large as 30,000 square miles. Despite the outward appearance of a Heath Robinson approach, these floors became temples of care and precision as photogrammetrists shuffled about in their felt slippers creating their Meccano-like assemblies out of plastic sheets.

The extra space allowed Hotine to accommodate other experts

who could extract useful information from the large areas of RAF photography that the Directorate now had available. In 1949, the Secretary of the newly formed Committee on the Aerial Survey of Forests was accommodated at Bushy Park and spent a lot of his time extracting tree-cover information direct from air photography for Colonial Forestry Departments. He was soon joined by a geologist from the Directorate of Colonial Geological Surveys who became the nucleus of a photo-geological unit at Tolworth. As well as exploiting the ever growing library of aerial photographs, this unit also provided geologists with training in the use of aerial photography and liaised with cartographers over the production of geological versions of the Directorate's maps. In most cases, these were prepared as overprints to specially simplified versions of the Directorate's topographic sheets and were first produced in 1952. The complex nature of the overprinted information required very careful checking by a specialist before the maps went to print.

After the move to Tolworth, Professor Dudley Stamp, well known for his Land Utilisation Survey of Great Britain before the War, persuaded Hotine to provide office space for the Secretary of the World Land Use Survey, an initiative of Stamp's that had the rather grand aim of helping the rehabilitation of the world after the War. The initiative did not prosper and, in 1953, Hotine obtained Colonial Development and Welfare funds to employ the Secretary as a Land Utilisation Officer in the Directorate 'to carry out general research on the potentialities of air photographs for yielding land use information of practical value to Colonial governments and on methods of making this information readily available for land improvement schemes or for opening up fresh areas'. [1]

In 1959, the forestry and land use activities were amalgamated into a Forestry and Land Use Section, with its own Assistant Director, R G Miller, 'to continue and extend the application of air photography to the specialised needs of agriculture and forestry development'. [2] The work of the Section involved both active field work abroad, visits to overseas departments and lectures to training courses at home. All these activities stressed the value to be gained from careful interpretation of the air photographs. In 1965, the Overseas Pool of Soil Scientists was transferred from the Rothamsted Experimental Station to complete the gradual expansion of specialities within the Directorate. At this time, Tolworth was clearly seen as the natural home for these activities which depended so heavily on the new mapping that was being produced. Hotine and his successors, all vigorous proponents of the benefits of air photography, were willing and enthusiastic hosts.

These new specialists were scientists and had a slightly different, perhaps more logical approach to their work compared against their map-making colleagues. Martin Brunt was one such who had taken up his appointment in 1956. He found the centrally heated offices difficult to cope with in the afternoons and when his sister, a doctor, told him that the most efficient way of dealing with drowsiness was to have a quick nap, he resolved to adopt the procedure forthwith and stretched out on his large map cabinet for ten minutes each afternoon. One day, however, the inevitable happened – the door burst open and in swept the triumvirate themselves, Hotine, Humphries and Wiggins. Brunt stated the obvious: 'I was just having a nap.' 'Quite so!' said Hotine. 'Now get down off there and brief us about your progress with the Gambia Rice Survey.' In this respect, Brunt lacked the skill of his senior colleague, Bussey, who was able to sit quite upright in his office after lunch, holding a pencil in the act of annotating a file, while in fact taking a quick forty winks.

In 1951, the Directorate welcomed another new group of employees. The recruitment of civilian field surveyors had continued to be a major problem and, in 1950, Hotine came to an agreement with the War Office to receive a number of Royal Engineers officers on two-year secondments for overseas work. By 1954, eight of the twenty-eight surveyors in the field were Army officers on secondment, and the Military Survey Service continued to supply personnel in this way until the 1980s. Army officers (and, later, non-commissioned officers) made a valuable contribution to the Directorate's work and had a considerable effect on the lifestyle of the survey parties that they joined. They were older and more mature and their two-year attachment meant that they often took a less obsessive attitude to the work in general. If they did not like the rules under which the field parties operated, they were more inclined to risk an alternative approach. Some took their wives out to the Colony. The more adventurous wives accompanied their husbands in the field. When a Director appeared on tour, the wife went off to stay with friends until the danger of discovery disappeared. Under Bere's austere regime in Morogoro, Tanganyika, one officer would push his vehicle out of camp after dark and drive 120 miles down to Dar es Salaam to see his girlfriend during her airline stopovers, freewheeling silently back into camp in the early hours without ever being discovered.

Almost from its beginning, the Directorate was involved in the mapping of Antarctica. The Colonial Office had asked it to support the Falklands Islands Dependencies Survey (FIDS) in mid-1946. In this way, the Directorate became the manager of the mapping programme, attempting to match the requirements of the scientists with the capability of the FIDS surveyors to produce the necessary ground control. In 1955, the Colonial Office placed a contract for aerial photography and ground control of part of the Graham Land Peninsula with Hunting Aerosurveys Ltd. The administration of this project, which presented some complex logistic problems, was entrusted to the Directorate, which used the resulting data to map the area. The mapping programme of FIDS, and later the British Antarctic Survey, remained the responsibility of the Directorate throughout its life and the unique landscape of Antarctica allowed the cartographers at home to exploit the full range of their artistic talents, while the maps that were produced added to the exotic quality of the corridor display.

These were heady days for the Directorate. Its capability had expanded slowly but steadily since its creation, and the new specialists had increased the range of its work. The 1945 Colonial Development and Welfare Act had provided the funds for a ten-year programme of work in the Colonies. When discussions took place about an extension to the programme, there was still sufficient political support for continuation to be approved. The only note of caution was a reduction in length of the second period to five years. In his submission for this new programme, Hotine acknowledged that less than half the mapping that had been forecast for the first ten-year period would in fact have been completed. This was because of the changes in priority that had prevented a systematic approach, the disappointing levels of recruitment of field surveyors and the demands for scales of mapping larger than had been anticipated. The new 1955 Act provided the funds that Hotine had requested and the next five years saw a small but steady increase in production resources. Hotine, in his role as Survey Adviser, retained the power to decide how he would spend his Annual Vote each year and to which applications for assistance he would give priority. However, by 1960, Harold Macmillan's Wind of Change was blowing through the Directorate's customers. Independence was on the agenda and new arrangements were soon to regulate Hotine's freedom of action.

PART III

NEW TERRITORIES AND THE CHALLENGE OF CHANGE,

1956–1965

Chapter 14

End of Empire

The move to independence amongst the Colonies of the Empire started with the Gold Coast (Ghana) in 1957 and accelerated considerably after Macmillan's famous speech in Capetown in 1960. Hotine had been quick to acknowledge the implications and he applied successfully to the Colonial Office for a change of name to the Directorate of Overseas (Geodetic and Topographical) Surveys in 1957. The newly independent countries moved from the paternalistic responsibility of the Colonial Office to a more austere and critical assessment by the Commonwealth Relations Office (CRO). Whereas the concept of a central service like the Directorate had fitted in well with the Colonial view of continuing responsibility, the CRO had quite different aims. It wanted to see self-sufficiency as quickly as possible and it set three conditions for Aid schemes:

- the recipient country should initiate formal applications for aid and should give a clear indication of the relative priorities of individual applications.
- the recipient country should contribute towards the local costs of each project as further proof of its importance.
- projects should be of defined and limited duration and should show some evidence of increased self-sufficiency on completion.

These conditions introduced, in the short term, the threat of serious dislocation to those projects which had already been started under Colonial Office control and were now being transferred to the CRO. In the longer term, they threatened the freedom and flexibility that Hotine had long enjoyed in deciding his programme of work and in allocating priorities to the numerous requests for aid that he received. These requests would now have to be channelled through a central department of the requesting government and would take their chance with other applications for new hospitals, roads, harbours etc. If bids were to be approved, local politicians and civil servants in every country would have to be converted to a belief in the value of national mapping. This had taken many years in the mother country and was unlikely to happen overnight in the newly emergent countries. A further difficulty would arise over the need for cash contributions until such time as local budgets had been arranged for the purpose.

Hotine was an enthusiastic supporter of training for self-sufficiency and was therefore very much in sympathy with the CRO's ultimate aim. Nevertheless, any time limits on projects, however well intentioned, made him very nervous, largely because of the high degree of weather dependence that all his projects had. If aerial photography was not obtained because of the whirling dust storms of an early harmattan season in West Africa, it might be a year before another attempt could be made. In such an event, he would be faced with a year's extension of the project but would also need to bring forward other work in its place to keep his staff occupied. A project by project approach jeopardised the commitment to a long-term programme which he needed for effective use of resources and which had been provided under the Colonial Development and Welfare (CD&W) Acts. To Hotine, the changes were unwelcome because they would introduce delay and uncertainty into the work of the Directorate. To the CRO, accepting the existing arrangements meant accepting responsibility for a large pool of permanent civil servants engaged on one type of Aid project. This would constrain its future ability to respond to the choices of emergent territories for particular forms of aid. This conflict of views delayed any decision on how to handle the work in hand at the time of the transfer of responsibility.

No projects were in operation in Ghana at the time of its independence and there was no difficulty in agreeing a new scheme of limited duration for the mapping of an area of 54,000 square miles and the training of Ghanaian surveyors. This was arranged under the UK/Ghana Mutual Technical Co-operation Scheme. However, mapping in Cyprus had to be suspended at independence because the Cypriot Government would not agree on its own cash contribution. It believed that a better deal might be achieved by delaying – the British War Office had a strong interest in seeing the mapping completed and might increase its funding if the delay became serious. In Somalia, the new Government saw the local cash contribution as a blatant attempt to recover as much of the aid as possible after independence and flatly refused to pay. Here too, work had to cease.

At the time of the negotiations on independence for Nigeria in 1960, the Directorate had four schemes in progress in various parts of the country. Far more resources were involved and it would be much more difficult to accommodate any suspension of work. Hotine became worried about the lack of progress six weeks before independence was due but, at a meeting with the Commonwealth Relations Office on 19 August 1960, it became clear that the Office would not agree to any work continuing until it understood the extent of future projects and had had an opportunity to obtain formal comments on the whole programme from the Federal Government in Lagos. This introduced further delay and, as late as the evening of Independence Day itself, the Directorate had to send a telegram to the High Commission in Lagos containing instructions for the surveyors working up-country. The Colonial Office Imprest Account was to be closed with effect from the previous day and they were to await instructions as to how the rest of the work was to be financed thereafter. There was an assurance that they themselves would continue to be paid but they were left to guess what to do about their locally employed staff. [1]

The difficulties over Nigeria led to a meeting with Treasury and CRO officials at the end of October to establish a set of principles to govern the Directorate's operation. To Hotine's satisfaction, the meeting agreed that, whereas there might be five to ten years' work left for the Directorate if it were confined to Colonial territories, there would be at least ten years' work if it also accepted requests from emergent territories. Temporary arrangements were agreed for the funding of this work in the short term. The longer term would now be affected by the recent recommendations of a House of Commons Select Committee for a pool of experts for work overseas and for a merger of the Colonial Office and the CRO.

It was not until early December that the CRO formally agreed to fund the Nigerian projects and then only until 31 March 1961. It insisted on a 15 per cent cash contribution from the local Governments and expressed the view that, looked at as a whole, the Aid programme to Nigeria had too much survey work in it and was, as a result, unbalanced. Though Hotine argued that many non-survey projects were being individually funded by CD&W funds after independence until completion, it is clear that there was a feeling that Hotine's direct contacts and warm relations with Survey Departments generated more requests than were the norm in other sectors. This anxiety was to grow over the years to come.

Hotine took the opportunity to assert his belief that operational efficiency should take precedence over financial constraint:

> I warned C.R.O. that there might well be difficulty in working exactly to the estimated appropriations and that I would be unwilling to divert production away from due priorities and economical working simply in order to square off the estimate. [2]

The Directorate was now funded in two separate ways: a large but declining part of its budget came from CD&W funds for work in the remaining Colonies; the remainder was to be earned through Appropriations-in-Aid from the CRO on the basis of work actually completed. In a brief for the Director's meeting with the Treasury in October, George Henlen, the Establishment Officer, had written:

> . . . it might be better and more simpler [sic] if a percentage of the total cost of the Directorate were to be met from C.R.O. funds. This would ensure that no great amount of clerical work would be needed to carry out the costing of all the projects and would prove simpler from all angles. In other words the Directorate would receive x% of its vote from C.D.& W. funds and 100–x% of its vote from the Commonwealth Relations Office vote. [3]

Simple or not, this approach had been rejected and there was a clear desire in the CRO to have much greater control over the programme and, indeed, the future of the Directorate. The uncertainty of the arrangements attracted Hotine to the Select Committee's proposal for a merger of the Colonial Office and the CRO. In a memorandum for the Cabinet Working Party which was looking into the question of establishing the new department, Hotine first set out the existing disadvantages. He went on to say that coming under the new department would have a significant benefit for the Directorate if it could then receive funding for work in dependent and independent territories, including non-Commonwealth countries, from one Parliamentary Vote. [4]

The new Department of Technical Co-operation (DTC) came into existence in July 1961, with the Directorate as one of its specialist units, but the challenges to the Colonial way of working continued. First, the Treasury demanded an annual review of the Directorate's activities and a calculation of the division of its resources between Colonial and emergent territories. It even questioned whether it should work for the latter at all. At the same time, officials in High Commissions abroad were also beginning to challenge the close relationship between the Directorate and local Survey Departments and to demand that all survey projects be subject to their approval rather than Hotine's.

In April 1962, K Christofas, the diplomat responsible for Aid in the High Commission in Lagos, made several outspoken allegations to a senior official in London:

> [I maintain] that a disproportionate amount of the limited resources available are [*sic*] being devoted to surveys to the exclusion of other more deserving projects. I also suspect that the Directorate of Overseas Surveys is deliberately touting for work in independent countries overseas (to be paid for by D.T.C.) in order to avoid the reduction of their existing establishment at Tolworth.
>
> . . . It falls on the joint shoulders of the D.T.C. and this High Commission to determine priorities for our technical assistance to Nigeria . . . I continue to believe that it would be useful if there could be a full and impartial examination by an economist of the value of surveys to the economy of a developing country, not in terms of absolute value but in terms of comparative value as against other needs . . . From the point of view of the impact it makes, survey work tends to blush unseen whereas the work of our better experts and our training programme is not only valuable but gains us considerable credit. [5]

This outspoken criticism ended with a challenge that the Institut Géographique National, the French Government equivalent, was doing similar work much more cheaply and the opinion that surveys should form about 25 per cent of the Aid programme rather than the present 37 per cent. In a second letter, he claimed that the Directorate work was going ahead without a formal request from the Federal Government.

The DTC acknowledged that this was so and that it was wrong, but claimed that it was pragmatic in view of the haste with which decisions had had to be made at the time of transfer. Later in May 1962, R B M King, a senior official in charge of finance, wrote to Lagos:

> In [considering its future activities] we have had it very much in mind that the Directorate being an organisation capable of giving useful technical assistance should be used to the maximum extent consistent with the

> demands which overseas Governments were likely to place upon it; and
> that we could only expect to keep the organisation going provided that we
> were able and willing to recruit on permanent and pensionable terms . . .
> We are convinced that we should only be justified in supporting the
> organisation insofar as it could satisfy the requests of overseas
> Governments within the amount of money we have available and bearing
> in mind their priorities for other forms of technical assistance. [6]

A rolling five-year plan from the Directorate would, in future, be
sent out to High Commissions for confirmation before it was
approved.

When Lagos asked for costs of projects in the current year, as a
base for establishing the trend in future years, Hotine finally saw the
DTC file and was irate, especially over the charge of 'touting'. He
immediately fired off a letter to King:

> I am frankly appalled at the situation revealed by this file. Christofas
> seems to have suffered, and to be still suffering, from quite a lot of
> delusions which might have been dispelled if the facts had been got from
> me sooner. [7]

He responded vigorously to the criticisms of the Directorate:

> I am afraid that it is all too clear that Christofas is hopelessly prejudiced. I
> have no confidence that he will impartially present to the Federal
> Government the five-year plan . . . . I think he should be given an
> immediate and crisp answer on the information which I have now
> supplied above, before his prejudices harden still further. [8]

King, however, suggested that a better course would be to invite
the official to Tolworth during his forthcoming visit to London.
This allowed the Directors to deploy their formidable secret weapon
– hospitality.

On arrival at the new Headquarters, the Directors had requisi-
tioned a room in which the carpenter had been instructed to build a
small semi-circular bar. It was named 'The Sub-Tense Bar' – a pun
on a piece of survey equipment – and it even had a 'pub sign' painted
for it in water colours by a Director General of the Ordnance Survey,
Major General J C T Willis. Later, when the room was needed for
more productive work, it was moved to a corner of the Conference
Room. Here, every lunch time, the Directing staff would dispense

beers and pink gins to themselves and any visitors, whilst discussing the latest aberration by some politician, Whitehall civil servant or Directorate surveyor. Those visitors who had come to complain were, more often than not, won over by the charm and unusually boisterous and friendly company. The more difficult ones might require an extension to the lunch hour at the local public house, the Queen Adelaide, but most found themselves on the train back to town with warm feelings of satisfaction and admiration for the indefatigable triumvirate and their organisation. Christophas was no exception. He wrote to Hotine by hand from his club on his return:

> I would not like today to pass without my writing to renew my thanks for
> all the kindness and hospitality which you and your Deputies showed me
> this morning. I found our discussion most stimulating; and it was
> extremely agreeable to have the opportunity of chatting afterwards over
> so pleasant a lunch. [9]

Nevertheless, the change in the manner of disbursing aid still stood. Instead of making allocations by sector and then leaving experts like Hotine to spread the aid around the Colonial Empire, it would now be allocated individually to each country and each country's Government would decide how to spread its allocation. The three Directors' enormous experience of the mapping needs of both the Colonies and the emergent territories could no longer be used to set relative priorities on the basis of an overall assessment. It was politically inevitable but it was the first crack in the Directorate's future structure and marked the beginning of a period of increasing regulation.

Chapter 15

Contours and Computers

Regulation from Whitehall was accompanied by increasing regulation within the organisation during the 1960s. The main reason for this was the search for greater productivity. It was inevitable that, as managers grew in experience, they would want to define and encourage effective procedures. For many, however, there was a sadness that some of the idiosyncratic ways of doing things were on the way out. Even after fifteen years, the Directorate used very few forms. There were, for instance, no printed forms for recording observations and surveyors were free to design their own layout on simple graph paper.

Map specifications, for long developed as the job went along, were an early candidate for regulation. A distinctive house style had emerged at an early stage and it was clearly sensible to build on this to establish a basic specification which would provide the starting point for discussions about mapping new territories and which could then be tuned to individual circumstances.

The three territories in East Africa had tried to adopt a common specification in the early 1950s but had failed to agree. With the Directorate's encouragement, a second attempt was made in 1958. To begin with, there was a feeling amongst the local Directors that they alone should define the specification and then the Directorate should adopt it for all future work. Wiggins maintained strongly that they had to take account of the methods of production used at Tolworth if they were not to compromise the effectiveness of the production line. There were difficulties in deciding on a vegetation classification suitable for all three territories but final agreement was reached in October 1962. It had been a hard-fought argument but the result was a design which was to serve as a model for map specifications for countries as far apart as Swaziland and Ethiopia. Encouraged by this success, the Directorate went on to develop similar standards for Nyasaland, Brunei and East Malaysia. These new specifications involved two more colours – this was an indica-

96

tion of increasingly sophisticated demands from users but had an impact on production rates. It was now essential for maps to be examined in the field, before publication, to ensure that road classifications and administrative boundaries were correct and all settlements properly named. Such 'field completion' was the responsibility of the local survey department and its timing was outside the control of the Directorate.

Increasing user demand also led to special one-off maps for tourist purposes. The first appeared in 1957 for Mount Kenya and was followed by several West Indian islands. These maps allowed the cartographers at Tolworth greater freedom to express their artistic talents. They laid the foundation for the increasing reputation of the Directorate for clean, modern map design.

The density of settlement in some of the more populated countries was now beginning to make the original 1:50,000 and 1:25,000 scales inadequate for urban and rural land use purposes and a demand arose for 1:10,000 or, in some cases, 1:2,500 scales. Although it could be argued that these were strictly outside the original concept of the Directorate's mission, Hotine's earlier freedoms had allowed him to take on the first tasks in Cyprus (1:10,000) and Malta (1:2,500) in the late 1950s and there was little difficulty in extending the principle to the West Indies in the 1960s. Many of the smaller countries lacked the capability to do the work themselves and it made sense to use the central facilities of the Directorate in this way, just as was done for smaller scales of mapping. The introduction of large-scale mapping into the programme brought considerable change to working procedures in its wake. The technical requirements were more rigorous, more sophisticated plotting machines were required and the field work was more closely specified.

One of the complaints that dogged the Directorate over the years was the time that passed before any maps were received by its customers. Complaints from professional users were founded on the common belief that drawing a map from an air photograph must only involve some simple and quick tracing operation. By contrast, more knowledgeable customers in local Survey Departments were irritated by the lack of any contractual commitment to delivery dates. The Directors shrank from such deadlines so as to retain the greatest flexibility of response to changing priorities or setbacks in, for example, the air photography programme. Obviously, one country's advance was another's setback. Furthermore, there was a growing problem with field completion. Local departments often lacked the funds to send a team into the field to check road data and add place names. Serious delays could build up at this stage and the Directorate had very little ability to influence the outcome. There was always considerable pressure to reduce the time taken by the production process. Luckily enormous strides were being made in the supporting technologies. Photography, microwave measurement and computing were three obvious examples.

In 1953, changes in the structure of the RAF and the withdrawal of the Lancasters led to a switch to the formerly disdained private sector for air photography. Expertise in the leading companies had steadily improved and, with the tried and trusted Dakota aircraft as their main platform, they were now capable of flying parallel straight lines of photographs just by eye. These were much easier to use than the circular arcs produced by the RAF, while the elimination of the radar stations removed a further source of potential problems and delays. The companies initially used cameras of British manufacture but soon went on to use Continental equipment with superior lens design. These cameras produced much sharper images from which more information could be extracted more easily. This in itself was a major economy because it was possible to use fewer, smaller-scale photographs to cover each map sheet and so reduce plotting times. The RAF had made a magnificent contribution to post-war mapping in Africa but its own interest in photography was for rapid reconnaissance and, as the demands of the map-makers became more sophisticated, the change was inevitable. In eight years, the RAF produced photography covering a total area of 1.1 million square miles.

The Directorate had opted for a separation between observing and computation in its triangulation work. The surveyors carried out minimal checks in the field and then sent their results home to be processed by a small group of highly specialised mathematicians who to put it very simply, had to solve very large sets of simultaneous equations in very large numbers of unknowns. One of the largest tasks consisted of 3,000 equations in almost 500 unknowns. The calculation of the coefficients for each unknown in these equations required intense concentration and hours of hand-cranking of calculating machines. The values for the trigonometric functions of angles were obtained by interpolation from published tables in which they were quoted to eight decimal figures. Errors were easy to make and very hard to track down. Simply recording the calculated coefficients on enormous sheets of paper required great care. Through the amount of work they undertook, these human computers became very skilled at what they did and world-renowned for what they achieved. Among their many successes, the recalculation of the East African triangulations as a coherent single network based on the Arc of the 30th Meridian and the derivation and introduction of a new projection for the countries of East Malaysia were perhaps the most important.

The advent of the electronic computer removed much of the strain from this work. In 1960, the Directorate was able to obtain time on the new Pegasus computer installed by the Military Survey Service at Feltham. The computational work was gradually transferred to this machine and its ICL successor over the next few years. Initially, there was a great deal of programming to be done but, in time, this investment paid off and the computer greatly speeded up the work of the Section.

As the Directorate accepted more and more requests for contoured maps, the provision of accurate heights assumed greater importance. Here too, there was a need for productivity gains. Complex procedures were simplified so that the number of heighted locations needed from the field was significantly reduced. The simple assumption that rivers in their lower courses generally have a steady gradient allowed heights to be interpolated along their length and this reduced the need for measured heights from the field. More significantly, Vic Williams, the Chief Photogrammetrist, persuaded Harry Brazier, the Chief Computer, that it might be possible to replace the tedious mechanical adjustment of the air photographs to ground control by a series of mathematical calculations joining one stereo-view to the next. This led, by 1964, to the method of Aero-triangulation by the observation of Independent Models, a development of major significance to the mapping industry as a whole and one ideally suited to the era of the electronic computer. Although it was being developed concurrently in other countries, it was in the Directorate that it was first seriously applied to the production process.

The achievement of Williams and Brazier, both production managers, is interesting when set against a statement in the 1948 Annual Report:

> Care has been taken to avoid over-organizing research. A separate
> research section would have to be small, would remove incentive from
> everyone else and might well get out of step with practical necessities.

Instead, anyone is invited to submit ideas and to work on them in or out of office hours; and trials are carried out by the normal machinery of production. [1]

Nevertheless, a Research Officer, Tony Eden, had been appointed at the start in 1946. Much of his early work was concerned with incremental improvements in the production processes. His main interest lay in photogrammetry and he pursued ingenious ideas for improved rates of production. In the computer era, however, his preference was for a more mathematically rigorous approach than that of Williams and Brazier but the pragmatic, production-oriented method of the two production managers was preferred.

Eden was much loved by all those who worked with him. He was kind, gentle and rather deaf and sometimes gave the impression of a classic, absent-minded boffin. It is alleged that, on hearing that he had secured a post at Bushy Park, Teddington, he promptly bought a house at Bushey, Hertfordshire, thinking he would be next door. An early car owner, he was prone to reporting its loss to the police when unable to find it in the car park in the evening, only to discover that he had left it at home in the garage or outside the local newsagent's shop at lunch time. He inspired great loyalty and enthusiasm amongst the photogrammetric operators who were assigned to him to develop pilot production procedures. Their strong sense of commitment could, on occasion, produce apparently viable production rates during trials which then could not be matched in routine work.

Nevertheless, many improvements were introduced during the late 1950s and early 1960s and there was greater standardisation in procedures throughout the organisation. Manuals were written for the individual map specifications that had been agreed for different parts of the world and, in 1965, work finally began on a Manual to regulate the work of the surveyors.

Beneath all the regulation, there continued to be a happy and friendly atmosphere and a social life still flourished. The average age in the drawing offices was about twenty-five and there were many evening and weekend activities which were always well supported. A Club for Activities and Recreation (DOSCAR) flourished with affiliated clubs for archery, badminton, cricket, football, golf, photography and table tennis. Arts, hobbies, handicraft and gardening shows allowed the staff to display their many and varied talents. Every Christmas, there was a very popular children's party. While surveying jobs were still very much a male preserve, there had never been any discrimination in the recruitment of cartographers. One result of this was that, in 1960, it was reckoned that there were twenty-five married couples working at Tolworth who had met as a result of working at the Directorate. The FIDS surveyors, back from working in the Antarctic, were always a source of excitement but one girl was more than surprised when she overheard a loud conversation in the VIP toilet next door to her office:

> The Governor of the Falkland Islands had come to see Hotine and, shouting as the Directors always did when they were in the toilet, he told Hotine that I would not be at the Directorate much longer as I was going to marry Derek Searle. I was not only miffed but alarmed, as Derek had never given any indication at any time that this was in his mind and, as he was just about to get back to the relative civilisation of the Falklands after two years on an Antarctic base, I thought he would be completely turned off if he heard the rumour. So I wrote and told him what Governors and Brigadiers were talking about in toilets in London and he was sufficiently annoyed to tackle the Governor on his return and extract an apology from him. [2]

Naturally, after all that, they did get married and lived happily ever after!

Chapter 16
Measuring the Land

The increased emphasis on contoured map production and the advent of the Tellurometer changed the field operation significantly in the 1960s. Whereas much of the earlier work involved laying siege to mountain tops and sitting out the problems of weather, the emphasis was now on speed of movement. In the years of urgency, the attitude was that the surveyors should get what they could as quickly as they could and the staff at Headquarters would do their best to find a solution. Maps with small errors were better than no maps at all. Now, emphasis on production efficiency led to more precise definition of what was required by the photogrammetric experts at Headquarters. The surveyors were left with fewer choices and, if there was a need for data in awkward terrain, they had to go in regardless.

Developments in photogrammetry meant that the number of positions to be fixed in the field was reduced but locations were conditioned more and more by the photography. The positions of flight lines were now carefully planned and the aircrew fully briefed on the requirements before leaving London. This advance planning lead to significant savings in the cost of ground control. All ground control had to be identified to within a few feet on the aerial photography by the surveyors. This could be quite difficult, especially as not everyone has perfect stereoscopic vision. There needed to be a fairly obvious pattern of vegetation around the chosen control point which could be detected with confidence on the photography. It was often surprising how much detail was visible on a clear photograph taken from a height of four miles but, in featureless terrain or with photographs taken through haze, it was easy to become confused. In West African rain forests with complete tree cover even on mountain summits, it was usually necessary to measure out to villages several miles away before an identification could be made with confidence.

There were two stages to the field work. First, the Tellurometer was used to fix a network of hill tops much closer together than in the primary triangulations – a spacing of 12–15 miles. Then a denser network of heights was established, using sensitive aneroid altimeters, to provide the information needed for plotting contours. The demand for increased accuracy in the late 1960s meant that altimetry was gradually replaced by more accurate measurements from prominent hill tops by Tellurometer but altimetry remained in use in forested country where visibility was restricted.

The amount of theodolite observation was much reduced and far less weather dependent. At the distances involved, opaque beacons were visible in good conditions, or well-focused observing lamps could be used as targets in overcast weather. There was little need for light parties to camp out on hilltops. The Tellurometer was provided with a two-way telephone so direct communication was possible between stations. Any difficulties that were encountered could be discussed on the telephone and the uncertainties of Morse communication were eliminated. Because, in most cases, there was now no need to camp on the hill, the surveyor could travel light and LandRovers became a more favoured mode of transport. The aim was to get in to a hill, complete the work and get out in a day wherever this was possible. The concept of what could be done in a day was, of course, stretched and the walk back to roadhead could become a weary trudge in the dark:

> Left hill at 1600. Saw three rhino on the way but they turned and went off into the bush. Met 7 elephants. Got lost! Reached Mwangazi at 1930 suffering from thirst. Dug hole in sand and found water. Continued down Mwangazi for about 7 miles. Arrived, exhausted, at camp at 2230 after making detour to avoid disturbing small herd of elephant at water hole in the river bed. [1]

In the dry season, tents were often left behind so that a LandRover could be used to carry a team in as close as possible to the selected hill. Tents often gave a ridiculous sense of security when lions were padding around outside yet they were abandoned without much thought. This might have been because increasing experience had made the bush as familiar as Oxford Street and a safari no more difficult to arrange or survive than a day-trip to London. Or perhaps it was the undeniable magic of going to sleep under a tropical sky with its myriad stars across which satellites now frequently traced their regular arcs. There were, inevitably, moments when it seemed to be a bad mistake:

> We had gone up the Zambezi from Feira in a small police boat and had had to travel light. We landed upstream of one of the river's gorges and there were not many flat places on which to camp. I had just a small camp bed and, rather ridiculously, blankets, sheets and pillow. (These were the standard issue.) I asked my cook to set up my bed on an elephant trail, which was wide enough and conveniently clear of scrub, on a high bank about 40 yards back from the river. I gave it no more thought than pitching a tent in the Highlands of Scotland. It was a clear night and, after the usual wondering inspection of the stars overhead, I fell asleep. The next thing I knew, it was dawn and my cook was whispering urgently: 'Bwana! wake up! wake up! there is elephant wishing to pass!' I have never got out of bed so quickly before or since. The elephant was 100 yards away proceeding steadily towards us on the path. Feeling something of a fool for choosing so exposed a spot to sleep, I managed to retrieve the situation by grabbing an empty jerrican and beating it. Hearing the noise, the elephant obligingly abandoned his idea of an early morning drink and padded off the way he had come. [2]

The heighting work could be even more demanding as there was a wider distribution of points required. Walks of 25 miles in a day were common. While the surveyor was out walking, two base altimeters were read by local employees at fifteen-minute intervals throughout the day at locations of known height above sea level. This allowed the surveyor's readings to be adjusted to sea level as well. However, readings at the base stations could be interrupted by wild animals or periods of bad weather, or the base reader could be delayed in reaching his location. There was no radio communication and there was always the possibility that the 25-mile walk might have to be done again because the base stations had not been operating through misfortune or misunderstanding.

Height points were required at the four corners of the overlaps between selected pairs of overlapping photographs. These overlaps were selected at intervals in every strip, usually in adjacent positions so that the working areas lay in bands across the countryside. Much depended on how these bands related to the available road network. If a surveyor was unlucky, there could be a lot of unavoidable walking. A common pattern was a rectangular walk around the overlap with side lengths of 6 and 3 miles. If you did two in the day, the distances covered could get quite large. Arnold Bloomfield went on one such trip in the famous Selous Game Sanctuary in Tanganyika in 1958. He first walked 25 miles into the Sanctuary from his roadhead. On the next day, to save the porters from following him around the rectangle, Bloomfield described a rendezvous to his headman from an inspection of the aerial photographs and the headman led the porters across the short side of the rectangle and made camp in readiness for Bloomfield's arrival:

> 18 January: All my local labour went home this morning, said they
> couldn't stay any longer; so left with my 18 'regulars' again. Sent them to
> a rendezvous, which I identified on the (aerial) photos and which
> the game ranger said he knew, to make camp. John, Abdu and
> I did altimetry, went very well too. And we met the others as arranged,
> and we found water. When we got here a herd of elephants were bathing,
> we scared them – but they scared us too![3]

The next day did not work out so well and, after a morning spent doing altimetry, he reached the day's rendezvous to find no porters and no camp. He went off and did some more heighting but, by evening, it was clear that something had gone wrong. The three of them were now without food or tent. They were 25 miles in from the road and had another clutch of points to observe, further in, the next day. Bloomfield did not relish abandoning at this stage and having to walk all the way back in at a later date, so he decided to try and finish the work the next day and to walk out to the roadhead by the end of the following day. It turned out to be too much:

> 20 January: Slept for 6 hours, surprising because the flies, ants,
> mosquitoes gave me hell. Up and off at 7.00 after a drink of water.
> Reached the far side of the last photo strip. Got mixed up with lots of
> elephant again and had a nasty face to face with a cow buffalo and her calf
> – not pleasant company. We managed quite well for water all day up till
> now, just ½ bottle left. Won't get back tomorrow, too far.
> 21 January: Intermittent sleep on side of large ant hill (fortunately vacant
> of tenants) because it had a convenient tree on top – just in case of
> emergency. Got to first (altimeter) point at 8.45, only 1 remaining. After
> reading felt faint, had to sit down again. Gradually got going to the last
> point, John and Abdu following. Had to skirt around a herd of buffalo,
> then got to the point – beside a water hole – great joy. Bathed and drank,
> called to the others but no reply. Worried after an hour, and decided we

had somehow missed each other when crossing a valley. They had my
gun and altimeter, I only had compass. Walked north-west all day, found
water periodically. Towards evening, thought I saw the beacon on top of
our base hill, but great disappointment when I got nearer, it wasn't.
Climbed up a hill and made bed of leaves on top of a rock, with a black
mongoose as bed mate.

22 January: Lots of hills all around, chose one to south-west hoping it was
our base. Arrived at top at 9.00, saw the beacon, collapsed on it in sheer
joy. Went slowly down to camp site at bottom, full of anticipation – but
nobody there. Grief beyond description. Found one inch of cassava root I
had thrown away before as rotten – ate it. Then found 1 lemon in similar
condition also bag of salt, empty sack and a small amount of meal that had
been spilt on the ground. Made porridge with meal scraped into empty
corn beef tin with plenty of salt – helped to restore strength. In evening a
severe thunder storm with heavy rain, so crept into sack for shelter.

23 January: Reckoned I was 6 hours from road. Eventually came out at
midday, as luck would have it near an altimeter base, still manned by
faithful base reader; remainder of my men had gone to the Police at
Mahenge. 'Missing surveyor' had been reported far and wide, and was
picked up by couple in car going to Mahenge much to their delight – and
his. [4]

This exploit will be (and was) seen as foolhardy by some. Bloomfield
was lucky to survive four days without food; one more setback
might have been the end of him. Yet his overriding determination to
see the job through, rather than lose time by walking out and
returning on a second and safer occasion, is typical of the attitude of
most surveyors to getting the job done. He may have taken his
determination further than many others would have been willing to
do but there was never any doubt that work took priority over
family, the bright lights, weekends and anything else. A mixture of
idealism and physical challenge was the driving force, and delays
were to be avoided at any cost.

However careful surveyors might be, there was always the risk of
natural hazards. Tropical storms were frequent and there was neither
comfort nor safety to be had in a tent during them:

Shortly after we reached camp, it started raining and then it happened: a
lightning strike hit the camp. I was in the tent when I was suddenly
knocked backwards onto the bed, a streak of lightning running up my leg,
sudden and excruciating pain and then tremendous noise. I tried to get up

but couldn't. There were screams outside in the camp. I had the impression that my leg was shattered to pieces. Eventually, I crawled out of the tent to see bodies sprawled about everywhere. As it turned out, no one was killed but 7 men apart from myself were injured. Since the driver was alright, I told him to drive us to the mission in Oban. It took a while to find the dispenser but eventually we were patched up. The labourers firmly believed that it was *juju* and refused to go back to the camp and I had to leave them at the Police Station for the night. Next day I took the injured to hospital: 2 chaps with badly burned legs, one with scorched back, one scorched side and arm and 3 remaining ones with scorched legs. My legs had burns and were swollen and I was suffering from slight deafness. [5]

During the dry season, fire could be a hazard as it swept through orchard bush, feeding on the light forest and long grass. Theoretically, the defence was to set your own fire and walk onto the burnt area as the wind swept the fire forward. When the real fire arrived, there was nothing left to burn. In practice it could be very different and very frightening:

At about 0400, I awoke to hear the crackling of a fire. I went out of my tent and could see some small fires over 100 yards to leeward, the wind was blowing over the top of the ridge and was blowing the fire away from us. At 0500, the fire was still moving away. An hour later, the headman called out that the fire was approaching. I decided that we could probably save the whole camp. Grass and branches were cut down to try and make a fire break and tents were taken down and everything piled in the centre of the camp area. We halted the fire on the side it had approached from, but it worked round the hill and we had to fight it off to the east and north, concentrating on keeping an area of 10 feet diameter clear. We stood in the centre of the area rushing forward to dash out advancing flames before having to retreat from the heat.

We would have won the fight but for another fire lower down the hill on the windward side; the wind was carrying the smoke from this in great clouds across the hilltop. I had made no allowance for this in my calculations. One man fainted, I caught another who looked as if he might run off the edge of the rock, everyone was coughing. Breathing grew more difficult; we could see nothing but smoke and fire. The two labourers ran off, my headman stayed a little longer before he made off too; by that time (with only my cook and I fighting the fire) some of my bedding had started to burn and, as we couldn't hope to succeed on our own, we had to follow the rest.

Under the trees, the leaf fires were relatively small and we got through or over them until we came to an area where the fire had already passed and sat there for an hour or so on the branches of a low tree. We tried to get back to the camp site about 0830 but food tins were still exploding so we left it until about 1000 when we removed the few items that were not too hot or too damaged. We left the hilltop about 1100 as we had to get back to Kainkordu that night to get some food and somewhere to sleep. The worst burns and cuts were sustained on the journey down from falling burning branches or from having to cross areas of still hot ash (some had no shoes). After 5 hours' walking (this being quite an effort as most people had burns on feet and legs), we got a lift by mammy wagon to Kainkordu. We last saw the hill about 1815 and it was still marked by a great plume of smoke. [6]

The 1960s saw the Directorate, with a slow but steady increase in resources, expand its sphere of operations away from a focus on African territories to the West Indies and the Far East. By 1966, parties were operating in sixteen territories from British Honduras to the Solomon Islands and from Kenya to Botswana. Each month, reports from all these parties would arrive on the desk of the Deputy Director. This post was now occupied by John Wright who was recruited from the well known private sector firm of Hunting Surveys Ltd when Humphries took over as Director from Hotine in October 1963.

He could be faced with a whole range of problems from across the world. In British Honduras, an abnormal rainy season had almost brought work to a halt and surveyors were complaining of wading up to their necks in swamp. In Botswana, there was a serious drought and the surveyors had to borrow a 1,000-gallon water bowser to survive in the desert. Once the Bushmen knew of the presence of a travelling water supply, they would arrive with their ostrich shells and make serious inroads into the reserves. In Kenya, the pillars that marked the survey stations were being removed by the Masai and, in the far north-east of the country, surveyors could only proceed with their work under police escort, two of whom were killed during a skirmish. In Sarawak, it was river canoes and rapids, trees and traditions that held up work in a country that had no significant road network. Up river, animist beliefs prevailed and if a hornbill flew from left to right in front of a line of porters setting out from a longhouse, that might put off any further travelling for several days.

A common problem in most parties at this time was the reliability of the early models of the Tellurometer. Some training in elementary fault finding was given to surveyors on leave but the faults that occurred in the bush always seemed to be much more obscure than those that were simulated in London. There was no local service network to speak of and delays while instruments were shipped home for repair could be severe. Wright decided to recruit two electronic engineers to provide regional servicing facilities in the main areas of the Directorate's operations. The engineers quickly became very knowledgeable about the equipment and gained the confidence of surveyors. Soon they were undertaking tours away from their regional centres and servicing the instruments of local Survey Departments too. A flexible attitude by both employer and employees allowed them to acquire surveying skills and they gradually transferred their contribution from electronics to full-time surveying as later versions of the instruments became more and more reliable and less and less in need of their attention.

This was a good example of an initiative from Headquarters improving the performance of field parties but, in general, it was not easy for the Directing staff to influence the pattern of events overseas. For most of the time, they were thousands of miles from the people they were trying to direct. Surveyors tended to have strong views and had the enormous advantage of being able to disappear into the bush if they wanted to cut themselves off from Headquarters' instructions and advice. Some surveyors, by the nature of things, were less enthusiastic than others. When Chris Bere, the East African party leader who had inspired a generation of surveyors in East Africa with a mixture of terror and respect, was promoted to an Assistant Director post at Tolworth, he found the distance barrier intolerable. Fretting at the difficulties reported by the Sarawak party, he decided to fly out and, in a short visit, show the surveyors how it ought to be done:

> I would expect to be either on one of the hills or travelling between them during all the hours of daylight; I would not wish to arrive at a longhouse mid-day or early afternoon only to be told that there were no labourers available until the next day. I understand that, given sufficient notice, the district officer in Tatau could arrange with any of the longhouses for men to be available at any particular time and day required. Alternatively, one

of our own labourers could be sent ahead travelling by whatever local
boats are available. I would not expect to reach any particular longhouse
at dusk each day and would expect to camp either in the longboat or in the
jungle on the way to the hill. I do not wish to sleep in any of the
longhouses![7]

I am a little concerned by your complete lack of camp equipment. My
policy has always been to get on with the job with as little delay as
possible, to live as comfortably as possible while doing the job but to
accept hardships cheerfully when they are necessary. If it is necessary to
go without a tent or a comfortable bed I am quite willing to do so, but I
am by no means convinced that it will be necessary. You have written off
all your canvas baths but I see no reason why I should not have a hot bath
as well as possibly a cold one in the river![8]

Naturally, he completed his planned programme within 24 hours of
the original schedule and, on departing for London, left behind a
rather breathless group of surveyors.

Each field party leader had his own way of organising the field
work, even if it did not always match Bere's efforts. Significant
savings in time could be achieved if return visits to inaccessible hills
could be avoided. A three-man team was a good balance between
efficiency and available resources and they had to plan to reach three
different hilltops at the same time on the same day. In some areas,
this was quite easy to arrange but, in difficult and remote country or
in the Pacific Islands, it could be a complicated logistic exercise and
needed careful planning. In Zambia, where local headmen had been
trained to carry out some of the work, one party leader evolved what
became known as the 'Z-plan' in which the individual schedules for
six surveyors and headmen for the whole month would be set out,
with the days and times each was required to switch on his
Tellurometer on each hill he was to visit. Built in to the plan would
be walking safaris, opening up tracks for LandRovers to reach
otherwise inaccessible hills, finding places to cross major rivers by
canoe, clearing hilltops and so on. Although much mocked by those
who had to endure them, the complex plans were surprisingly
successful, probably because their very complexity somehow inspired everyone to keep to the schedule. After all, it would get so
very much more complicated if a date was missed.

Directors also had occasional personal requests from surveyors to
deal with. Harry Green wrote from Northern Nigeria for advice
about a worm which was living in his sub-cutaneous tissue and had

started to move across his eyelid. In the absence of any reliable medical opinion close to his base, what should he do? Back came a less than reassuring telegram: 'Your worm is bizarre but harmless.' Green was never one to let small worms interfere with his work and stayed on until he went home on leave. He was one of the most dedicated field surveyors that the Directorate employed and he won the hearts and the admiration of many young surveyors sent to spend their first tour of duty under his careful guidance. During his career, he was involved in the field operations for some 250,000 square miles of 1:50,000 mapping – nearly three times the area of Great Britain.

National mapping was now well advanced in many territories and more and more requests for large-scale urban mapping were beginning to arrive. In 1959–60, the output of the Directorate was some 300 sheets of mapping at 1:50,000 or similar scale and the only completed large-scale task was the revision of the 1:2,500 series of Malta. By comparison, in 1969–70, 39 per cent of the total map output was at large scale compared with 31 per cent at 1:50,000. This change in emphasis produced a number of tasks covering towns or small development schemes. In such cases, a presence in town was an unavoidable necessity rather than something to be avoided at all costs. If they were lucky enough to find housing, surveyors could work from home every day and return home in the evening to a bath and a cold drink – and, for some, to a wife and family as well. It was certainly a more regulated existence than in the days of geodetic and national mapping projects but it was not always uneventful:

> Had a bit of excitement in a village last week when some idiot killed a small boy with a shotgun thinking he was a monkey. Naturally, the crowd wanted to matchet [sic] the man with the gun but as my observations were right in the middle of the riot I had to do something and managed to grab him and carry him off in the LandRover with the mob pounding on the windows. I took him and his victim into the town to the Police barracks and the Hospital respectively. The child was still alive despite the choke barrel's contents in the back from about 20 yds. He died later and over 70 pellets were extracted at the autopsy. [9]

However, while some were leading a less eventful life in town, others, caught up in the expansion of the Directorate's work to Malaysia and the Pacific, were having to learn the less familiar skills of travelling to work by water.

Chapter 17

It Helps if You Can Swim

Most surveyors had some experience of climbing mountains and of living in tents before they came to the Directorate. Few had similar experience of travelling by water. As the work of the Directorate expanded geographically, so an increasing amount of it depended on water transport. The rivers of Borneo and the islands of the West Indies and the Pacific all demanded adequate boats for the job. The constant pressure to economise on transport, the high cost of boats and problems of availability meant that it was not always possible to obtain the most suitable – and sometimes a surveyor's impatience to get on with the job meant that risks were taken.

In Sarawak and North Borneo, there were few roads in the 1960s. Transport inland was by river canoes, powered by outboard engines. On the placid lower reaches of the rivers, the canoes were 40 feet long and fitted with neat little roofs along their whole length to protect the passengers from sun and rain. Towards the front, travel was quiet, comfortable and exhilarating as the narrow canoe sped smoothly through the water. Unfortunately, when going upriver against the current, actual progress could be very slow. It was not unusual to spend forty-five minutes going round in a large meander only to have moved 50 yards in a straight line. Further upriver, open, shorter canoes were used as the rivers became shallower and rapids became a problem:

> While negotiating a tricky rapid near a huge fallen tree on the Sungei Paong, the engine stalled and we were swept against it by the current. So strong was the current that before anything could be done the whole boat was sucked under the tree and immediately split down the centre and broke up. Some of the equipment remained within the tarpaulin which was still attached to part of the boat and was saved in a few minutes. The rest of the heavier things sank in the deep, swift flowing water. However with persistent diving, quite a lot was recovered including the 10 hp outboard engine, the fieldbag containing the air photographs, a barometer

and several smaller items. Our worst loss was food as we were only able to recover some rice, which got wet and quickly went mouldy, and 3 small tins of fish. We were not able to cook that night as matches were soaking and attempts at rubbing sticks failed. However, the next morning with the sun and the aid of a stereoscope, we were able to light a fire and cook a small meal.

We then set about building two bamboo rafts and by 1300 were able to set off floating back down the river with occasional exciting dashes down rapids. Only on the following afternoon and feeling very hungry did we reach the first habitation where we were able to get food and a lift down to our main boat at Lepu Leju. [1]

In this case, the surveyor was on a reconnaissance. The worst time to experience a sinking was on the way back from a spell of observing, with all the observations and other information that had been acquired by hard graft over several weeks. This did occur on one unfortunate occasion when a month's work was lost and had to be repeated.

The smaller rivers up-country could rise and fall up to 40 feet in a day, depending on the rainfall. When they were in flood, these rivers could be quite hazardous with strong currents and a lot of debris. The boat would be travelling at treetop level and could easily be snagged and turned over by unseen obstructions.

Whenever there was a need to take the river canoes from one river system to another, there was the problem of a short sea journey. The canoes were only seaworthy on a near calm sea and it was not easy to assess conditions without going out to look. The most serious problem was at the mouth of the river where there was a sand bar on which the slightest swell could create the most enormous waves over a short distance. The canoe's length exaggerated the pitching and, once committed, there was no turning back, for the canoe was at serious risk when broadside on to the sea. These lessons were often learnt by trial and error:

The first time we tried to cross the bar of the Oya River, we started taking in water over the bow. As those who saw what was happening were 30 feet forward of the driver, and the roof was in the way, it was difficult to get him to slow down and we were soon waterlogged. As one man, everyone bar me leapt out of the boat. I immediately assumed that they were looking after themselves. They would head for the shore and safety, leaving me to decide what to do about the Tellurometer and the rest of the kit. I was wrong – having sensibly reduced the load in the boat by their prompt exit, they clustered round it, yelling at me to bale like mad. This I did, whereupon they all clambered back in and we headed back into the safety of the river, with little damage to the equipment. [2]

Experiences like this led to the purchase of sea-going boats but even they had problems. This account of two such boats leaving the Mukah River is typical:

> *Seraya* (our inboard motor fishing boat) and *Seagoon* (our sea-going longboat with two outboard engines) were waiting at Mukah to make the short sea trip round to Oya. At 0700 I went out in *Seagoon* to check the possibilities of moving and found that the sea was not as rough as on previous occasions so we returned to Mukah to load. As the wind came up a little in the next hour, the *Seagoon* driver, Sambang, was instructed to take it steadily and to return to Mukah if he was doubtful.
>
> The sea was a little rougher than it had been an hour previously but Sambang still thought he could make it. However, after crossing two large breakers, he changed his mind and decided to return, but both engines were swamped in the attempt. One cut out and the other was insufficient to turn the boat; another wave broke over them and the other engine cut out. The men then jumped out and attempted to pull *Seagoon* in but could not so they abandoned it. All reached the shore safely.
>
> Meanwhile *Seraya* had got on to the sand bar and was temporarily stuck. Before we could get over to *Seagoon*, one engine broke loose from its transom and, as it was chained to the other [engine], dragged along the bottom and effectively anchored the boat. If this had not happened, *Seagoon* would have floated into shore with only minor damage, as did most of the kit on board. However, it started breaking up and would have completely disintegrated had not *Seraya* managed to reach it.
>
> For over an hour in a fairly rough sea, we attempted to get a line on the boat and eventually threw the anchor in, got a grip, and towed it into Mukah harbour. The two new 40 h.p. engines were still attached, but battered, and the [longboat] itself was in poor shape.
>
> Men were sent along the shore to recover the kit which had been washed up and we found everything except a nylon tarpaulin and small stores such as primus stoves. To add insult to injury we had two fuel tanks stolen after we had rescued them. The stores were strung out along 600 yards of beach and it was difficult to guard everything. The police have recovered a 5-gallon tank and are still looking for the 25-gallon one and a tarpaulin. [3]

The canoes in Sarawak were painted bright yellow to aid identification in an emergency – this was the time of 'confrontation' with Indonesia – and they were therefore easily identifiable. The surveyors preferred to employ Ibans from up-country because of their bushcraft skills but Ibans still carried the reputation of headhunters among the coastal people. On one occasion, these two facts combined with a local rumour to provoke unexpected trouble:

> The troubles began by a rumour in Sibu that the Government required a 'head' for the foundations of a bridge which allegedly was going to be built over the Oya River. This spread downriver to the Melanau populations living on Pulau Bruit and at Matu. It grew with repetition and this fact, combined with our yellow boats full of Ibans appearing unexpectedly, led to the belief that we were out to get the 'head' for the Government. The rumour that we were head-hunting spread rapidly and was followed by increasing hostility and open threats. We eventually decided to withdraw to Sibu for a while.
>
> However, the rumour went about Sibu that we had returned from downriver 'headless' and were now about to search in the Sibu area! This led to threats being expressed in town whenever our yellow LandRover passed the Kampongs and to deliberate damage to two of our boats. It is hoped that in a month or so, all will be forgotten and we can go back to Pulau Bruit and be welcomed![4]

Further east, in the Solomon Islands, there were different problems. Here the work covered a double chain of scattered volcanic islands, several hundred miles long. Small ships rather than canoes were the only means of travel and, for the surveyors, this meant coming to terms with the unfamiliar idea that they were not in absolute control of their means of transport, which in turn meant that they were not in control of progress on the task in hand. In Africa, where vehicles, horses or even small boats were the norm, the surveyor remained in control and could decide how far to push his transport before resorting to walking. In the Solomons, it was different; the captain of the ship, no matter how small, bore complete responsibility for the safety of boat, passengers and crew. He alone decided when he would sail, how long the journey would take, where he could safely anchor for the night, how close he could approach the shore or when he could cross a reef into the shelter of a lagoon. This meant a total reappraisal of working methods and a reluctant acceptance by the surveyor that he was only a passenger.

He could indicate on the chart the point he wanted to reach but the rest was down to the bosun, and there was no sense in becoming impatient or heavy-handed; a belligerent bosun could easily jeopardise the whole programme. The smaller ships could take more risks and come closer inshore; the larger boats always kept well away from possible trouble and sought safe anchorages for the night, even when this involved several hours' sailing away from the work area. In spite of the cautiousness of the crew, the surveyor took time to adjust:

> On the long passages, the seasickness and the occasional bouts of sheer terror were gradually overcome. I really did not think the boat would survive my first storm at night. Down in a trough, the bow would be engulfed in the next wave, 20 or 30 feet high, until the boat struggled free and perched on the crest before sliding down into the next trough. It was all very different to my first idyllic view from the aircraft as we came into land – then everything had looked so perfect, the forest green of the mountainous islands fringed with yellow sand and set in a sea that changed from blue-black to azure to light blue as the plane crossed the reef and flew past a lagoon on its way in.
>
> The Solomons were always a contrast – so much that was breathtakingly beautiful yet the heat and humidity were very enervating and most of us suffered from skin diseases, ringworm, boils and carbuncles. In my last two years, I lost over three months' work through illness – malaria, skin diseases and deep leg ulcers which seemed to go on for ever. One of the Mission stations became quite famous for its ringworm cure – a mixture of meths, kerosene and neat iodine which converted skin to black leather after about two applications. The patch usually fell off after a week or two, leaving, if you were lucky, clean new skin underneath![5]

The sea was not always hostile. Every surveyor experienced days when the idea that someone was paying you seemed ridiculous and it was often at sea that perfection and contentment were encountered. One evening in the West Indies, the survey party used a local schooner service to return home to Anguilla from the French island of St Martin:

> At first, the vessels made their way accompanied by a chorus of animated shrieks and giggles from the young girls as they recounted the exploits of the day: all this against a deeper background of talk lubricated by the wine

that had been drunk in St Martin. Slowly, as the three schooners approached the Anguillan shore, low against the evening sun, the noises ceased until only the lap-lap of the waves and the crack of the sails disturbed the evening quiet. And then gradually the unmistakable sounds of West Indian hymn singing filtered across from one vessel to be taken up by its neighbour until all were mouthing or humming in a perfect harmony that reflected the Welsh origins of the early settlers. Against a changing background illuminated by a crimson sun and a sky darkening to display a myriad stars, our feelings were only of harmony and humility. [6]

Chapter 18

Wives Join In

The ban on wives accompanying their husbands abroad continued until 1956. Unfortunately, there is now no record of why it was then lifted. Some of those affected suggest that it was the result of a Treasury ruling. Others say that it was simply an admission that something had to be done to slow the rate at which experienced surveyors were resigning. The new arrangement meant that married surveyors could take a wife out on every second one-year tour – most married couples, however, opted to stay abroad for two consecutive tours. There seemed to be little enthusiasm for the change amongst the Directors. Little was done to prepare wives for the culture shock that they were about to experience. Nothing was done to adjust the way of working or the living conditions. Wives were expected to adapt to the situation. The work was not to be delayed by their presence.

The first wives to arrive, therefore, found themselves, within a day or two of leaving London, living under canvas in a base camp with a group of bachelor surveyors who had until then enjoyed a clubby, male existence. There was little privacy and the bachelors were not always thrilled to have to adjust their way of life to accommodate the presence of a woman. Once ensconced in base camp, there were two options: go everywhere with your husband and accept the rigours of safari life, or endure the boredom and isolation of an empty base camp while the men were away. Sometimes there was no option: the logistics of a foot safari into a waterless area, or of a long sea voyage, might not allow the presence of an extra, non-essential person. Party leaders were insistent that married status could not excuse a surveyor from the more difficult assignments and, indeed, it sometimes seemed that married men got more than their fair share of the physically demanding jobs.

Marjorie Ayers was married to a Royal Engineers officer who was posted to Uganda in 1958. She went on every trip with her husband in spite of the initial culture shock:

Within a few days of arriving in Entebbe, I was off up country in a battered Bedford truck clutching my Swahili phrase book. On board were tents, table and chairs, bedding and three enormous wooden boxes containing cooking pots, <u>china</u> crockery, Tilley lamps and so on. After a night in the relative comfort of a rest house, we set off on foot into the uninhabited Elephant Sanctuary, casually ignoring a notice that said it was dangerous to leave the safety of the vehicle. I found the first night under canvas truly terrifying, with what seemed to be every conceivable animal making its contribution to the strange sounds of the African night. Next morning, our headman, Musuoka, explained to me that the loud scratching sound I had heard had been an elephant just outside my tent.

We would walk up to twenty miles a day and the most unnerving part was moving through elephant grass taller than any of us. On one such occasion, Musuoka suddenly stopped dead, turned round and, eyes wide, whispered to me 'Great danger!' Just ahead of us was a lone buffalo. We all turned tail and ran. Musuoka lost his sandals and I quickly realised that stylish rope-soled espadrilles were no footwear for such occasions.

If we had to cross a river, Musuoka would carry me over on his shoulders while my husband led the party across what he hoped would be the shallowest route. The possibility that there were crocodiles about could never be ruled out. On one occasion, an elderly man was brought into camp with a ghastly gaping wound in his thigh from a crocodile. Having only Dettol available, I poured it neat into the wound, wrapped it up as best I could and took him off to the local dispensary in the lorry. [1]

Wives often earned their keep – recording observations for their husbands, helping with the paperwork or going off to replenish food stocks when the work dragged on. Joyce Morris spent twenty-four years roaming the world with her husband. Even on her first tour to Kenya, she was soon into her stride:

Down on the Tana River, it was rain, rain, rain and the work was going too slowly. We were running out of food so another surveyor, Charles, and I set off in a LandRover to get more food from Galole. 15 miles out, we stuck in black cotton soil up to our floorboards. We then set off to walk the 12 miles to Galole, it being the shorter option. There were the noises of wild animals all around and we were lucky to have a full moon for we didn't arrive until 10 pm.

We went to the Club and found three expatriates who entertained us for the rest of the evening and put us up for the night. Back at camp, Geoff was a little concerned but his colleague felt it did not justify interrupting the work so they went out as usual the next day. In the evening, Geoff insisted on going to look for me. He passed the LandRover still stuck where we had left it and found us back at the Club again and still having a good time. 'Come on in and have a drink!' was the cry. What else could he do?[2]

Soon came the daunting prospect of bush pregnancies. The uncertain timings of these events could lead to difficulties. The official insistence that the work must go on meant that there was little sympathy with the idea of the husband staying in town for the last few weeks to make sure he was available when needed. When Liz Lynch needed a dental check at seven months in Botswana, she took a lorry for the 300-mile journey across the desert from Maun to Francistown and then the train to Bulawayo on her own. Although by this time the families had acquired housing in Maun, Liz had no transport of her own. The night before she gave birth, she had to walk to another wife's house in the dark to get a lift to hospital. In this party, the wives operated a base radio link to the surveyors so her husband did know what was happening very quickly. Some years before, one surveyor was unaware of the birth of his first child for four days and his second for two.

Getting to hospital in time was often a problem and on one occasion, in Belize, things happened too quickly. Tony Weston and his wife Di were living 5 miles outside Orange Walk, itself 60 miles from the main hospital in the capital. There was some doubt about the date the baby was due but, a week before the earliest estimate:

Di started to have pains about 5.30 so we had an early breakfast and packed the LandRover ready to depart for Belize. At 8 am, the waters broke. I rushed our other daughter out into the LandRover, thinking we might still have time to get to the local Mission. When I got back, the baby was on its way. I managed to get a sheet down on the bare wooden floor and laid Di on it while asking her, as a nurse, for any instructions that might be useful. In the end, the baby came out so quickly that I was unfairly accused of pulling. I had time to work out that it was a girl before I had to worry about cutting cords and so on. By now, Di felt sufficiently recovered to want a better qualified attendant so she told me to tie the cord, help her up and take her to the local Mission doctor. It is not easy for one man to lift and carry a mother with her baby still attached but the local carpenter hove in sight and came running to help. The track was in bad condition after overnight rain and it took 25 minutes to travel the five miles to the doctor's house. He soon did all that was needed and I was quite proud of my performance when he charged me only $15 for his services instead of the usual $35![3]

New mothers were often quickly back on safari:

We took our second child into the Kalahari when she was just three weeks old. Life was far from easy. She was a baby that liked to scream a lot; I was unable to continue feeding her myself so, when she started screaming in the night, it meant leaving a warm bed for the freezing night outside, lighting a lamp, blowing up the embers of the fire and crouching over it to warm up the milk. Later on that trip, the seven year drought broke and it rained and rained. I remember the desperate attempts to try and dry nappies under a tarpaulin and having to squat on the camp beds as water poured through the tent.[4]

There were times when it could be quite frightening too:

One hot afternoon I put the baby down to sleep in one tent, tied the dog up to the tent pole and crawled into our second tent to have a snooze myself. After a while, the dog became very agitated and I yelled for him to shut up. He took no notice so I got up to see what the matter was. To my utter horror, an enormous snake had crawled into the tent and was raising its head at the dog who was going crazy. I untied the dog, grabbed the baby and ran screaming for the cook. He said it was very dangerous. The snake curled up under the bed and it wasn't until the men came back in the evening that we despatched it by collapsing the tent and pounding the canvas with sticks. It turned out to be a black mamba, over ten feet long.

On another occasion, I came across one of our hens with a foot of snake hanging out of its mouth. It eventually swallowed it and, later, we ate the hen![5]

However, while living out in the wild could be attractive and exciting, there could be real problems. Christine Leonard experienced perhaps the most dreadful tragedy of anyone in the life of the Directorate:

She was developing into a bright little girl – like quicksilver, people said – sturdily built, a clear sense of purpose and an uncannily philosophical temperament for an almost-three-year-old. A mild dose of hepatitis

diagnosed by the locum doctor at the Sapele plywood factory two days
before had led to a troublesome cough and Catherine was subdued as John
[Christine's husband] left on Monday morning for his week's work at
Warri. She was listless but bore the discomfort with predictable fortitude.
Evening brought no improvement – perhaps the morning would? But, as
I watched through the night, her condition deteriorated with frightening
speed into a high fever. At first light, we drove immediately to the doctor
and thence to the clinic at the factory. An increasingly desperate day sped
by in numb horror as, one by one, the doctor's efforts failed to overcome
the problems of a seriously ill child, at the mercy of a barely-existent
telephone service, inadequate facilities for anything more serious than
routine first aid and a country where nothing is achieved without a
preliminary 'dash'. By now barely conscious, she seemed entirely
dependant on the oxygen mask that I held to her face – the mask which I
increasingly knew to be her lifeline. Telephone contact was made and
suddenly we were to move – by car to Ibadan. I knew few people in
Sapele but remembered one who would, I knew, go to Warri to find John
– so a message was sent. Rushing out into the stiflingly hot and dark
night, carrying our precious cargo and an oxygen cylinder, now half-
empty, our journey began – a car, a boat, then another car. With
deepening dread, I watched as the contents of the cylinder reduced with a
speed unmatched by our painfully slow progress on the rough dirt road.
The driver, the doctor and I sat in leaden silence – the awful emptiness of
knowing the certainty of the outcome. Suddenly, the cylinder emptied
and all efforts to revive that brave little spirit were fruitless. It was over. [6]

Five days later, the Leonards flew back to a cold wintry England to
bury Catherine and, ten days after that, returned to Sapele to
continue their lives:

Strangely, we felt no sense of anger or blame – either at the inadequate
medical facilities available or the absence of expertise which might have
saved Catherine's life. Perhaps some anger at least might have made it
easier for our vociferously demonstrative Yoruba neighbours to
understand us, but we took the quieter and very 'British' path of
emotional self-control. And was this not predictable? Those of us who
served the Directorate (and this was very much the wives too, supporting
the adventurous spirit of their husbands) took the risks as part of our
commitment to a fine organisation. In those days too, the still-powerful
legacy of a wartime upbringing ensured that, even in the face of deep
personal loss, we should contain ourselves. Today, I know that we are

more able to expose our pain. Perhaps our Yoruba neighbours were right, after all.[7]

As time went on, the accommodation options improved. Houses which were either condemned or surplus to requirements were obtained from the local administration to replace the base camps. The furniture was primitive and the house would usually be occupied by several bachelors as well as the married couple. It did, however, introduce an element of normality into life for a few days at the end of the month. Many wives took on the role of 'mother' to the bachelors and standards visibly improved – better meals, a little more care over appearance, more social contact with the neighbours. If there was harmony in the house, the arrangement worked surprisingly well. However, this was always a matter of chance and, if a wife was unlucky, a new tour could change things for the worse:

> The house, which was lovely, was on its own over a long very lonely road. I was totally alone during the day with a small child and the days were endless. I can remember going down to the beach in front of the house and crying my eyes out many times. It was so desolate . . . So that was the end of DOS for me. Throughout my life since then, though, I have realised that I learnt an awful lot and, because of the life we led, I can cope with any situation. I still love camping and roughing it![8]

Now, in the 1990s, the attitude that wives then were mere camp followers may seem uncaring, even callous. It has to be seen, however, in the context of the times – both in terms of the attitudes towards women and of the sense of overriding urgency which still permeated the Directorate. Most of the field work overseas was unavoidably tough and that could not be changed. Directorate staff had no entitlement to housing which, in any case, was in short supply. The Directors had no alternative to offer married men; wives who went abroad could only make do with conditions as they found them. Some loved what they found; some put up with them in the hope that they would get better; surprisingly few packed up and went home. And their presence brought one undeniable benefit – their husbands began to think of the Directorate as a career and, at long last, the 1960s saw the number of surveyors reach the figures that Hotine had first thought necessary.

Chapter 19

Preservation and Propagation

The mapping process produces a host of documents which require storage, some for posterity, some for frequent reference, some to allow a second printing of a map when stocks dwindle. Everything from surveyors' field books through aerial photographic films to large negatives of the final map needs careful cataloguing and a decent environment. However, while careful storage and preservation was essential, it was equally important to publicise the existence of the material and to make sure that it was readily available to those who could benefit from it. These duties fell to the staff of the Records Section, later known as Technical Services.

At the beginning, responsibility rested with a Records Officer, Jack Bentley, who was also in charge of Stores. This was not entirely illogical as, at that time, the survey data for each country were kept in separate, large brown paper parcels lined up on wooden shelving. If a cartographer was working on Kenya mapping, he took the relevant parcels and signed for them as if they were theodolites or drawing sets. Eventually, a more sophisticated approach was called for.

The first changes occurred in the Survey Data collection in April 1950, when a cartographer in the middle of an advanced photogrammetry course was unexpectedly told in the corridor that he had been promoted and placed in charge of Survey Records. Chris Lovell's terms of reference were to devise a system whereby any survey point and the documents related to it could immediately be located. His ideas came from a most unlikely source. Before the war, he had maintained a stockbroker's card index, with a card for every company listed on the Stock Exchange. He worked through existing records that used the parcel numbers and, country by country, converted them to the classification system that is still in use today. In 1950, these records were listed in one black 'Kalamazoo' binder, by 1957 there were nine binders, and eventually no fewer than forty-nine volumes in two cupboards.

Wiggins took a particular interest in developing a map library and gave it a good start by using the same technique as he had with other stores. He commandeered a vehicle, went to an Army map depot and took whatever he could lay his hands on. He issued instructions that 'Records will maintain the map library in which two copies of every map should be filed'.[1] The map collection grew steadily; the intention was to make it comprehensive: 'Mr Wiggins is very keen that our library be as complete as possible with copies of every map ever made of the Colonial Territories.'[2]

Bentley retired in 1950 and returned to Nigeria, where he had business interests in Jos, and was succeeded by John Mankin, a surveyor with pre-war experience in Palestine. With the move from Bushy Park to Tolworth, Lovell records that 'the additional tasks of organising the map library, map stocks, books and periodicals and the storage of the "finished material" from the cartographic sections were thrust on me'.[3]

The largest expansion in the work of the Directorate in the period 1950–2 was in the Records Section; the numbers of both accessions and users increased, and reorganisation following the move to Tolworth was hampered by lack of staff: 'The whole system of indexing the working material, maps, reports, etc . . . requires overhaul . . . most of the weekly intake of prints (which is about 30,000) [is] not properly checked.'[4]

By December 1951, the quantity of work demanded a new approach and a committee recommended the establishment of a separate Records Section staffed by graduate geographers. The new structure under Tony Stickings came into effect in September 1953 and the new staff were able to provide a much broader service than simply cataloguing records. They handled public relations, documented progress on major projects and became more and more involved in the technical administration of the Directorate's mapping programmes as well as servicing the growing demand for the Directorate's maps, aerial photographs and technical data from private companies and consultants.

The Records Officer became particularly concerned with the contracts which were now necessary for the acquisition of the major part of the aerial photography. The Map Curators compiled numerous and comprehensive briefs for Directors on overseas tours. These were extensive and invaluable documents identifying current problems requiring action overseas and supplying background summaries of progress on current projects – as Douglas Warren was to say on his retirement from the position of Director many years later: 'After all, what self-respecting director can travel without his briefs.'[5] These briefs were based, as was so much of the work of the Section, on the detailed knowledge of work in progress that was built up during the procurement and evaluation of library material which, though provided primarily to support the Directorate's map production, had many other ancillary uses.

The storage of original aerial photographic films is a demanding requirement, needing carefully controlled atmospheric conditions as well as a high level of security, particularly from fire and water damage. This was a problem to begin with and, in 1955, the films were transferred to a deep, and not always water-proof, cellar at Thames House, on Millbank. By the following year, the films were being 'conditioned' in a special room in the Photographic Section at Tolworth. Here, in a relative humidity of 50 per cent, they were individually wound on special cores and sealed in new aluminium cans. The continual call on the films for further prints, the workload involved and breakdowns of the conditioning equipment led to the abandonment of conditioning in the early 1960s but storage at Millbank continued until the early 1970s, by which time an increasing number of films were being transferred to the countries they related to and only reference prints were retained at Tolworth.

Perhaps the most significant contribution of the Map Library to map production was the critical evaluations that were made of all the available information for a new mapping block. These might include everything from existing maps of varying reliability to press cuttings of recent construction projects. When map sheets were not sent overseas for field completion, this system ensured that any new map included all existing reliable names, road classifications, boundaries and facilities.

It was the aim of the Directorate to show international boundaries on the face of medium-scale mapping wherever they had been sufficiently well defined and there was enough information available to enable them to be drawn without significant error. To achieve this aim, a collection of printed and manuscript source material was built up and, to the considerable edification of the Colonial Office and local survey departments, exploited in the compilation of a series of dossiers describing the history and alignment of each boundary. By no means all British Colonial boundaries received the full treatment, but dossiers were prepared for an appreciable number of those in Africa. *Ad hoc* enquiries from the Foreign Office and itinerant boundary commissioners from Commonwealth countries were also handled with despatch and authority, so that a considerable reputation was built up over the years.

The broadening scope of the Records Section was recognised in May 1963, when it was renamed Technical Services and Ian O'Brien was put in charge of it as an Assistant Director (Mapping), with additional responsibility for the letting and administration of contracts for the acquisition of aerial photography, by then a considerable undertaking.

The size of the various Libraries grew year by year. In the Survey Data Library, the total number of files and field books catalogued up to 1984 exceeded 40,000. 180,000 survey control points were used in the map production process over the Directorate's thirty-eight years. The meticulous attention to detail, which was typical of the Section's work, was invaluable in 1982 during the Argentinian invasion of the Falkland Islands and South Georgia. All the original records of the Directorate's mapping of the islands had been carefully safeguarded and the Library was able to meet virtually all the many requests for maps, air photographs and survey data received from the Ministry of Defence, the Foreign Office and the media.

The Falklands were not the only focus of enquiries. As the Libraries grew to cover a greater and greater area of the globe, they became an increasingly useful source of information to commercial companies and to other Government departments. A list dating from 1970 shows the extent of recent enquiries at that time. Maps had been supplied recently to over thirty British government departments and official bodies, from the House of Commons to the Royal Botanic Gardens at Kew, and seven units of the Overseas Development Administration. Some twenty survey and construction firms made frequent use of the Directorate's services, inspecting maps, survey data and aerial photographs, and purchasing their requirements. The areas of main interest varied over time: for several years, Nigeria was a centre of developmental activities; later, it was the Yemen Arab Republic; or Belize; and so on.

One of the major factors behind the success of Technical Services over the years was the building up of a corpus of knowledge and experience by its long-serving staff. There were a number of changes in the mid 1950s, but from 1958 to 1984 the key posts were occupied by remarkably few people. This was, of course, a general feature of the Directorate. In this case, it was particularly useful to have such detailed knowledge of what had already been done and where it could be found. Cartographers at Tolworth as well as surveyors overseas were sometimes irritated by the attention to detail and an insistence on the creation and return of proper records of what had been done but, to their credit, Technical Services persevered. Its staff did a great deal to systematise the way of working in the Directorate. Their contribution was vital and greatly improved the efficiency of the organisation.

Nevertheless, however useful the Directorate's services might have been, and however impressed Royal and ministerial visitors during the 1960s were with the skill and enthusiasm that they found displayed, there were those in both the Government and the Civil Service who felt that the Directorate was becoming something of an anachronism in the post-Colonial world and who wanted to challenge its right to exist.

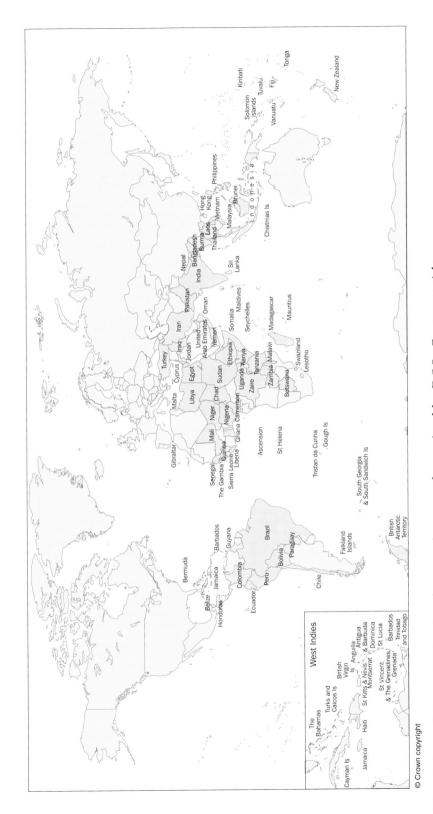

Map 1 Map of the world showing the countries mapped or assisted by DOS. *Crown copyright*

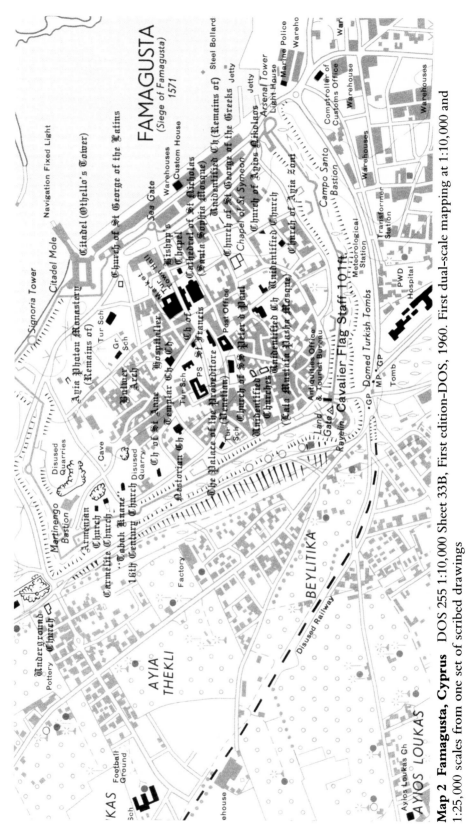

Map 2 Famagusta, Cyprus DOS 255 1:10,000 Sheet 33B, First edition–DOS, 1960. First dual-scale mapping at 1:10,000 and 1:25,000 scales from one set of scribed drawings

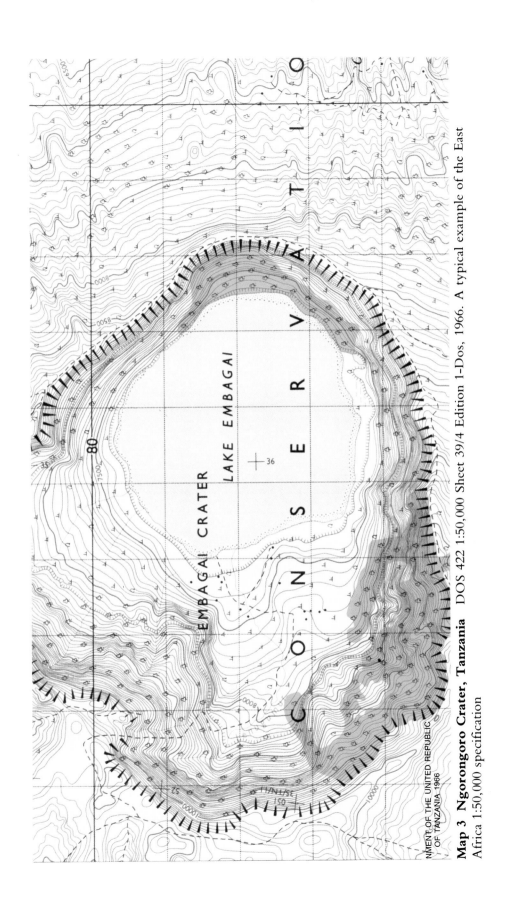

Map 3 Ngorongoro Crater, Tanzania DOS 422 1:50,000 Sheet 39/4 Edition 1-Dos, 1966. A typical example of the East Africa 1:50,000 specification

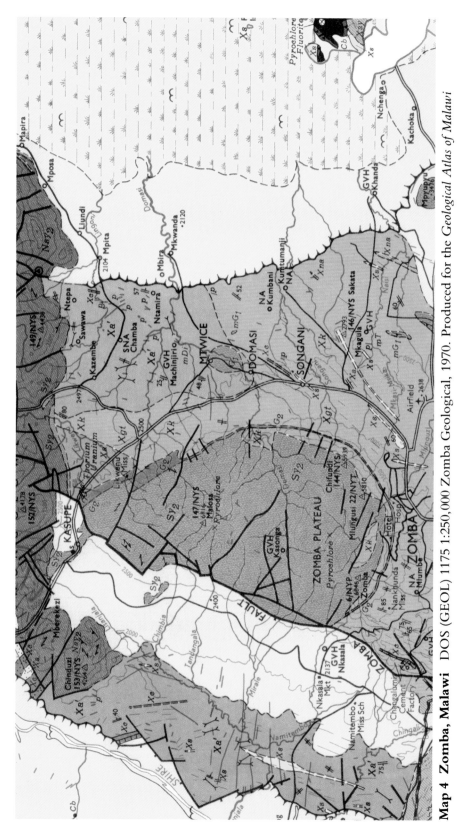

Map 4 Zomba, Malawi DOS (GEOL) 1175 1:250,000 Zomba Geological, 1970. Produced for the *Geological Atlas of Malawi*

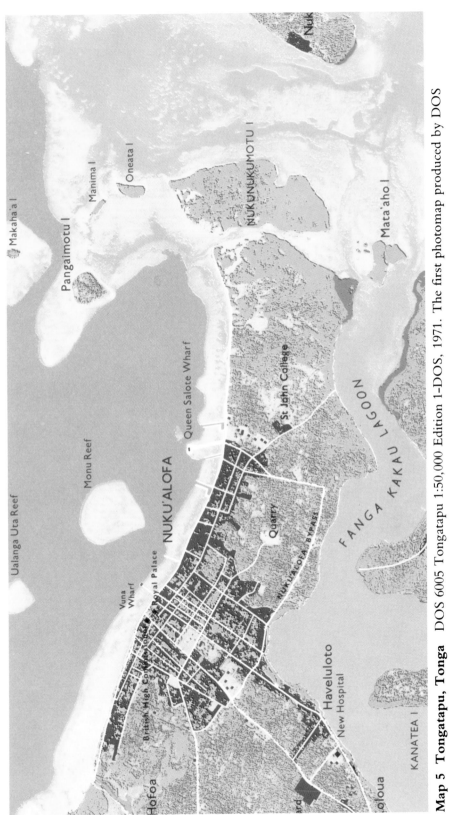

Map 5 Tongatapu, Tonga   DOS 6005 Tongatapu 1:50,000 Edition 1–DOS, 1971. The first photomap produced by DOS

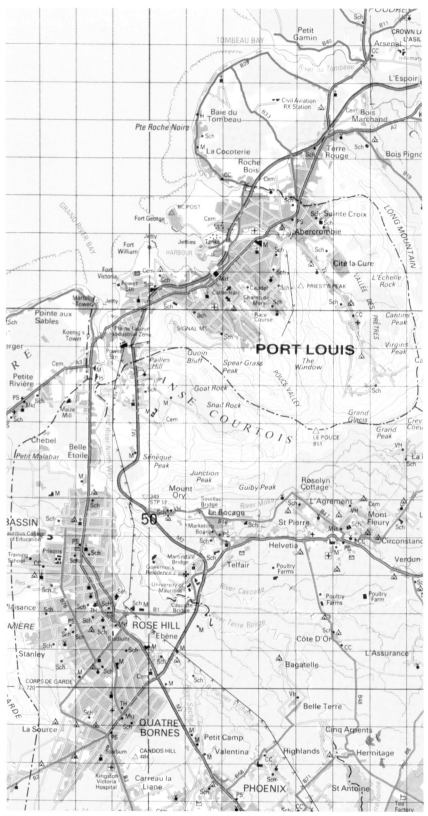

Map 6 Port Louis, Mauritius   DOS 529 Mauritius and Rodrigues
1:100,000 Edition 4–DOS, 1983. A derived map from the series DOS:
329, 1:25,000 of Mauritius. The attractive colour specification is marked-
ly different from that used on other DOS maps at the same scale

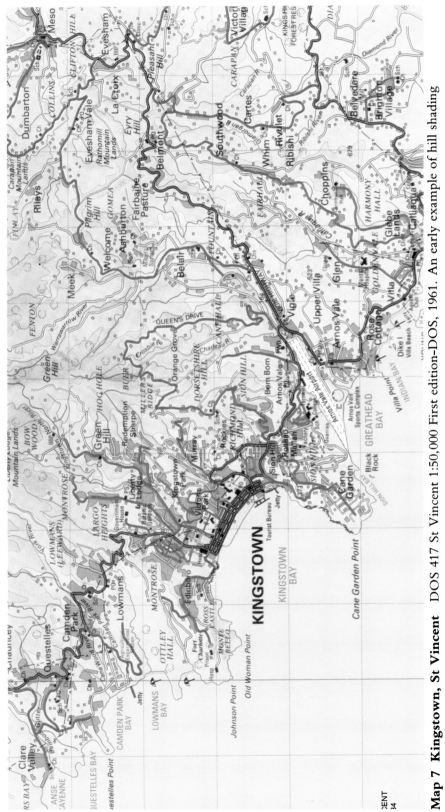

Map 7 Kingstown, St Vincent DOS 417 St Vincent 1:50,000 First edition–DOS, 1961. An early example of hill shading

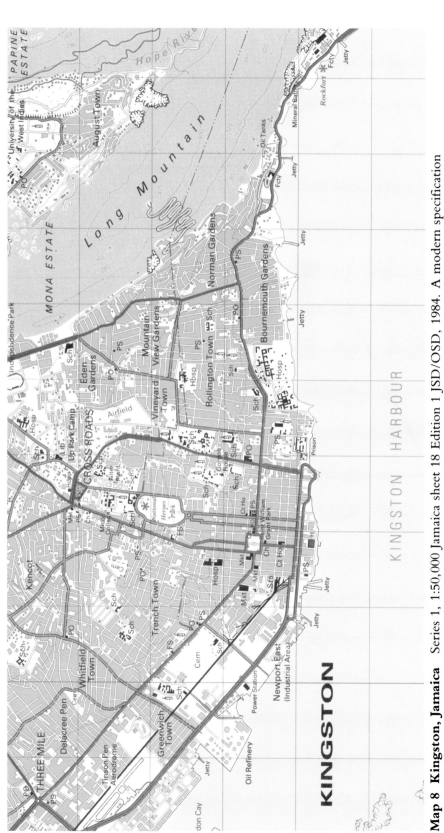

Map 8 Kingston, Jamaica Series 1, 1:50,000 Jamaica sheet 18 Edition 1 JSD/OSD, 1984. A modern specification

PART IV

POLITICS AND THE FINAL YEARS,

1966–1985

Chapter 20

Racked by Reviews

In 1964, a Labour Government came to power and signified the importance that it attached to overseas aid by creating a Ministry of Overseas Development (ODM) and giving its Minister full Cabinet rank. A White Paper in August 1965 introduced a more managed approach to aid, stressing the need to 'develop a long-term strategy for our aid, so that we do not simply react to past decisions and the pressures of the moment' and to discuss with recipient countries how aid should be provided and for what projects.[1] At the same time, ODM officials were seconded to High Commissions overseas to assess aid applications and, in 1966, a British Development Division was set up in the Caribbean for the same purpose. All these developments were part of the trend towards a more structured and centrally planned approach towards the granting of aid. The Directorate sat more and more uneasily within this framework.

The first serious challenge to its role came from an unexpected quarter. Experience on the new Military Survey Pegasus computer had convinced the Directorate's computing staff of the potential productivity gains to be obtained from carrying out all their work in this way. Wiggins, who succeeded Humphries as Director in October 1965, therefore submitted a proposal to ODM to buy a mainframe computer for the Directorate's own use. The Treasury, at this time, was very concerned about what it saw as an uncontrolled expansion in the number of computers in the Civil Service and all applications were subjected to a rigorous investigation. A team from the Organisation and Methods (O & M) Unit of ODM carried out this investigation and insisted on first considering whether the work of the Directorate was justified and, if it was, whether it was being done in an effective manner. It was thus a much wider-ranging investigation than Wiggins could have anticipated. It recommended that the fundamental role of the Directorate should be reviewed and that future commitments should only be accepted on the authority of the Geographical Departments in ODM. As for the computer itself, the workload was insufficient for a dedicated machine – the Director-ate should continue to use Military Survey facilities.

The outcome could not have been more disastrous from Wiggins' point of view. Instead of getting a computer, he was to get a major investigation into the justification for the Directorate existing at all. It was perhaps a case of an out-station failing to pick up the way thinking was changing in Whitehall but, at a meeting at ODM, he protested vigorously:

> It should be possible for one to have confidence that an O & M report would be both factually correct and objective. This draft report is neither. There is no hope of agreement being reached on the basis of this draft which abounds with errors due, I think, probably to Cooper [the leader of the O & M team] having attempted judgement on professional matters which professional men around the world are still debating. Of one thing I am sure, there would be unanimity among all professional men in condemnation of Cooper's attempts at professional judgement. The draft also abounds in misrepresentations of fact from the title and first paragraph onwards. [2]

Wiggins ended his statement by saying that the only solution was to suppress the draft entirely and write a completely new report under agreed and observed terms of reference. He failed to convince ODM officials that a new start was necessary and the review of the role of the Directorate went ahead in 1968.

However, the organisation still at this time enjoyed support at high levels in ODM. In particular, the Permanent Secretary, Sir Andrew Cohen, had been its strong supporter since Colonial Office days. He had been Governor of Uganda in 1952–7 and would have entertained Hotine during the latter's overseas tours. In 1962, Cohen had written during a tour of East Africa:

> Both [Tanganyika and Uganda] give very high priority to the continuation of the topographical and geodetic survey programmes, which they regard as fundamental to development. The Tanganyika Government wants the programme stepped up by 25% next year. Since the Directorate is one of our most developed means of providing assistance, we can welcome these requests, and I made this clear. [3]

When the review team met Sir Andrew, he told them he was 'anxious that nothing should be done which would disturb the efficiency of operation of the D.O.S.'.[4] With this encouragement, the team confirmed the Directorate's remit. It introduced greater control from the centre by recommending the creation of an Overseas Surveys Advisory Committee which would approve all new proposals in the light of their aid-worthiness and their relevance to the British Aid Programme as a whole. In addition, the review reflected current ODM thinking in its recommendation that the Land Resources Division should be separated from the Directorate and given a similar advisory structure of its own. The fundamental review of the Directorate's role was thus avoided with the help of some of the older ODM officials whose Colonial Service background made them more sympathetic to the value of the Directorate's services than younger colleagues who had had no administrative service overseas.

Approval of projects was now a much longer process and depended on the views of a number of officials. It was perhaps fortunate that the time for Wiggins' retirement came soon afterwards in May 1968. The new Director was Douglas Warren, who had served in the Colonial Survey Service in Tanganyika and Kenya and who had, for the last two years, been a Deputy Director under Wiggins at Tolworth. He had brought with him an understanding of the customer's view of the Directorate but, more importantly, he had not been part of the pioneering era. He therefore found it easier to accept the inevitable logic of greater central control than any of his predecessors might have done. The delays in decision-taking that were caused, on occasion, by this increased control could be very irritating to a Director worried about keeping his unit fully employed but Warren was pragmatic and accepted the need to make the system work. Indeed, in 1968, he appointed three Regional Survey Officers to work with some of the new regional Development Divisions in evaluating aid proposals, to provide a source of advice on survey and mapping to governments in their areas and to act as managers of all the field parties within the region. Warren's ability to understand the system and to work within it was crucial to the Directorate's continued existence during the 1970s. His style was utterly different to that of his predecessors but his logical mind and his willingness to conform to the changes required of him contributed as much to the success of the Directorate as Hotine's infectious enthusiasm.

Two important recommendations of the review team were later endorsed by the Advisory Committee. One extended the remit of the Directorate – projects could be undertaken in non-Commonwealth countries – and the other accepted that proposals for large-scale mapping, which were becoming increasingly common, could be a proper use of the Directorate's resources.

In 1970, a Conservative Government was elected, committed to reducing the role of government. A review of the appropriateness of all Government functions was announced and Overseas Development was downgraded to an 'Administration' within the Foreign Office (ODA). In 1971, a team from the Civil Service Department, under the chairmanship of a businessman, K F Lane, looked at the Directorate. They worked quickly and their recommendations were brief:

- The Directorate should no longer be a part of ODA – so that ODA would no longer be constrained in deciding the aid programme by its management responsibility for the Directorate.
- All survey and mapping aid should be put out to tender.
- ODA should appoint an independent adviser to evaluate requests for aid.
- The uncertainty of the Directorate being able to adapt itself successfully to a tendering regime was, in the view of the team, so great that it was preferable to close the unit down over the following two to three years.
- Overseas training could be handled by Ordnance Survey.

The Report clearly set out the criticism that had dogged the Directorate since the early 1960s:

> . . . the minimum size of the survey and mapping programme is
> determined once a decision has been taken about the DOS complement,
> because of the need to keep its staff fully employed. This in turn has meant
> that individual projects do not have to compete for Aid Programme
> funds, either with capital projects or with other items of technical
> assistance. [5]

The Lane Report was never published and Warren had to dispute its recommendations under a blanket of secrecy. He was helped by the fact that the Mapping Adviser to the team had filed a Minority Report noting the waste of goodwill and resources in closing the Directorate and recommending that the Directorate's programme for the next three years be recast into a series of projects which could be controlled more closely. The Adviser also wished to see a greater proportion of work being contracted out to the private sector.

With the help of colleagues at ODA and a crucial intervention by the Ministry of Defence, Warren succeeded in reducing the impact of the Report. In May 1972, it was announced that the Directorate would continue in existence for a further seven years but its future would be reviewed in 1975 so that decisions about any changes required in 1979 could be made in good time. The complement would be reduced by 25 per cent over the next two years and any mapping required in excess of its reduced capacity would be contracted out to the private sector. The total number of staff employed had reached a maximum of 490 in 1970 (with 500 local employees overseas). As a result of this announcement, the number declined to 346 by 1974.

The next review was not so long in coming and sprang from quite different political considerations. Sir Henry Hardman had been appointed to investigate the potential for moving Headquarters Units of Government Departments to regional locations to achieve a more even spread of Government employment opportunities. In 1973, Hardman recommended that the Directorate should be moved to Manchester or Glasgow. The proposed move, which understandably caused great concern amongst the staff, would not take place until the staff reductions and the review scheduled for 1975 had taken place.

The Labour Party was returned to power in February 1974 and returned ODA to full Ministry status. Shortly afterwards, a report by Lord Rothschild recommended that all science-based activity within Government Departments should have a sponsor department which formally commissioned the work and took some financial responsibility for arranging the funds for it.[6] As a result, ODM reconstituted the Advisory Committee as a Management Committee with the intention that it should carry out a much more rigorous evaluation of the Directorate's future commitments, in order to ensure that they conformed to the Minister's priorities for aid and thus could be seen to comply with the Rothschild doctrine. This process involved the Geographical Departments of ODM, overseas posts and Development Divisions. It was also expected that economists at the Ministry would co-operate with the Directorate to evaluate the role of mapping in economic development. While Lord Rothschild's intentions were both understandable and laudable, the result was a blurring of responsibilites and an increase in tension between the centre and the units concerned. The complex, time-consuming procedure of investigation and approval sat uneasily both with the urgency for mapping which often arose with a new development project and with the continuing need to have in place a programme of work sufficient for those employed in the Directorate.

In 1975, the expected review of the Directorate took place under the leadership of R H Belcher of ODM. The review team recommended that the Government should continue to provide technical assistance in survey and mapping through the Directorate, which should remain in being after 1979 without radical change. Although there would be a decline in requests for the Directorate's services during the 1980s, 'there would probably be a justification for about two-thirds of the present staff numbers into the 1990s.'[7] After several months of Ministerial discussions, the Government finally confirmed, in July 1976, that the Directorate would continue beyond 1979.

Uncertainty remained, nevertheless, and attention now returned to dispersal. The staff mounted a high profile campaign; there were serious staff losses and anxieties were expressed about the ability to recruit in Glasgow. The issue was covered in the press and on television, and an Adjournment Debate took place in Parliament in November 1976. There was much sympathy for the Directorate at ODM, typified by a letter from a senior official to Warren:

> I would not like to move on without saying how much I have enjoyed working with yourself and [your team] over the last three years. They have been years of exceptional difficulty for the Directorate and I have never ceased to marvel at the patience of you and your team in the face of Hardman and all that. But quite apart from the stresses and strains of the dispersal issue no one can have close dealings with the Directorate without forming the highest regard for its staff, whether on the field or the cartographic side, and their devotion to the work in hand.[8]

More delay followed and it was not until November 1977, four years after the original recommendation was made, that the Government confirmed its decision to move the Directorate to Glasgow. This long period of uncertainty had had a disastrous effect on morale. There had been a steady seepage of cartographic staff to more secure posts in the London area, especially to Military Survey at Feltham. Warren was deeply dejected by what had happened. He wrote to Hotine's widow in February 1979:

We are probably enduring the most unhappy time in DOS at present since its creation in 1946. The definite decision to move to Glasgow has been answered by the staff by wholesale resignations. We are now down to about 33 basic grade cartographers who can actually produce something out of a complement of 95. It is tragic to see such a fine organisation dying like this and it is of no personal satisfaction to me that I predicted the outcome right up the ladder as far as the Lord Privy Seal only to be told that I was talking rubbish. [9]

However, a Conservative Government came to power in May 1979 and promptly cancelled the whole dispersal programme, ironically rejecting the policy which had been set in motion in 1973 by a previous Conservative administration. The Directorate was to remain at Tolworth for the foreseeable future but its production capacity had been badly damaged by the inability of the politicians of both parties to make up their minds about the issue.

It had been a turbulent twelve years and it was an uneasy calm that returned in 1979. The new Government had again reduced the status of overseas aid, as the responsible department returned once more to the status of an Administration (ODA), though, on this occasion, retaining its independence. The debate about the value of survey and mapping in the aid field remained unresolved. Was it sufficiently fundamental and important to justify the Directorate's privileged access to aid funds? Were the arguments that the Directorate was an efficient, dedicated and reliable converter of aid funds into results still valid? For how long would senior officials in ODA continue to support its existence? The original timescale for mapping the Colonies laid down after the War had been far exceeded. The reasons were convincing at the time and had seen the Directorate through every crisis since, but the political scene was changing fast. There was not long to wait before the answers arrived.

Chapter 21
Training for the Future

In spite of perpetual anxiety over the many reviews that took place during the 1970s, this was a productive and innovative period. The Directorate adjusted its way of working to reflect the closer involvement of Ministry officials and the requirement for well-argued project proposals. It placed greater emphasis on training in the field and it used new administrative opportunities to second staff into local departments for training purposes. It increased the number of countries for which it worked and took on a wider range of projects in those countries. There were improvements in techniques and innovations in map design.

The Annual Reports show that work was undertaken in one form or another for an average of around fifty countries in any one year. Much of this work was designed to encourage self-sufficiency. Local surveyors were attached to field parties to gain experience in control surveys. In countries as wide apart as The Gambia, Botswana and Guyana, where the flat nature of the terrain led to requirements for accurate heights by precise levelling techniques, teams of technicians were trained up to continue the work independently of further external supervision.

In 1964, a scheme referred to as 'Home Base' had been started to release a supply of experts from UK Government Departments for secondments overseas as part of the Aid Programme. The Directorate made much use of this opportunity and, by the 1970s, one third of the surveyors were on secondment to overseas governments. Their duties varied widely: members of Land Adjudication teams in the West Indies, District Surveyors in Sabah, Chief Surveyors in the Solomon Islands and the British Virgin Islands, Survey Advisers in the Yemen Arab Republic and Indonesia and Project Co-ordinator in Mauritius. These jobs were often more sedentary than the occupants were used to or indeed wanted but, for many, they provided a welcome opportunity for a more stable family life. In nearly every case, the aim was to train a local candidate for the post. This was not always successful if the job involved a significant element of field work. It was common to find that, in a developing country, greater status attached to office-bound jobs and that these attracted the more competent and ambitious applicants. This led to difficulties in recruitment and longer timetables for self-sufficiency. The Directorate itself was sometimes criticised for failing to bring emerging Survey Departments to a state of self-reliance more quickly. It was inferred that there might be an element of self-interest in maintaining dependence. Many inside the organisation, however, argued that the problem lay in the poor status that land surveying enjoyed in the minds of local people leaving higher education.

Cartographers and photographers also came into the 'Home Base' scheme as the years went on. This was mainly due to the efforts of Warren who accorded them far more status that the original triumvirate were wont to do. To the original Directors, cartographers had little else to learn than the use of a drawing pen. By force of post-war circumstances, they used very basic methods and they were regarded very much as 'other ranks'. Warren, however, introduced modern methods of map production, encouraged cartographers to experiment with these methods and to specify the work required from the field surveyors. He was very willing to send the best ones overseas. Several worked in local Survey Departments and some were involved in the Joint Projects that were developed in the late 1970s.

They proved to be excellent ambassadors for the Directorate's policy of practical aid that produced results. Typical of the impact they had was Laurie Bryant's assignment in Pakistan in 1978. Despite overseas training by other donors for members of the staff of the Geological Survey, the difficult climatic conditions in Quetta had prevented any map production since their return. Bryant arrived with his personal baggage full of the printing chemicals required and rapidly had the presses rolling and maps printed.

It was perhaps natural that the schemes for attaching local surveyors to field parties and for seconding Directorate staff to local departments should eventually be brought together in a single concept. The opportunity arose when John Wright, one of the two Deputy Directors, went to Addis Ababa in 1969 on other business and, by chance, was invited to visit the Ethiopian Mapping Agency. He found an organisation with many of the resources already in place in terms of equipment and staff. What was needed to get things moving was an injection of expertise in map-making procedures.

Discussions began on a possible joint project in which both organisations would be involved in all stages of the map-production process. The Ethiopians would take on more and more responsibility as the work progressed. There was strong support from the Embassy and from ODM and a Memorandum of Understanding was signed between the two countries in December 1970. Joint Project Managers from Ethiopia and Britain were appointed and twenty-five surveyors and seven cartographers served on the first and second Projects over a period of eight years. The Agreements contained clear target dates for completion of the mapping, meeting a criticism that many had made of the Directorate over the years. It was also agreed that half the mapping would be produced in Ethiopia.

The field work presented many challenges in terrain that rose to nearly 14,000 feet and was heavily dissected by valleys up to 5,000 feet deep. The high plateaux were covered in black cotton-soil which became quite impassable to vehicles during rainy weather. Roads were few and far between and one annual report recorded the use of lorries, LandRovers, mules, ancient DC3 aircraft and a ferry consisting of an inflated sheepskin as transport during the year. The surveyor who took advantage of this last recorded the event in his monthly diary:

> Start at 0600. Decide it would be quicker to cross Gogeb by ford
> especially as locals tell us that there is a man with an inflatable boat. Arrive
> at ford and look for boat. 'Boat' turns out to be a strong local swimmer
> and an inflated sheepskin. Cross river by clutching sheepskin and lying on
> back in water to act as ballast whilst swimmer rides on top clutching
> survey equipment and propelling craft by breast stroke kick. After 20
> crossings all personnel and equipment are across. [1]

The Project was affected by political changes in Ethiopia and the Revolution complicated work both in the office and the field. In 1976, a surveyor had to withdraw from working in the mountains and, during 1977, there was a gradual run-down of surveyors until they were finally withdrawn in October 1977. Two years later, it was decided that the field work could safely restart but, four days before the first surveyor was due to arrive in Addis Ababa, the Central Planning Supreme Council cancelled the Project. No explanation was ever received.

In spite of this unsatisfactory end, the Project had been a real success, unlike previous attempts by other Aid agencies. In the first

Project, the Ethiopian Mapping Agency staff plotted 53 of the 88 map sheets; in the second, they produced 65 out of 69. But success should not be measured in material outputs and the transfer of expertise alone – one only had to meet the Ethiopian members of the project to realise how much the close working relationships had done for mutual understanding, respect and friendship – 'outputs' that are perhaps overlooked in the economic assessments of cost-benefit. Similar projects were negotiated in Sudan, Liberia and the Yemen Arab Republic though the extent to which maps were produced locally varied from country to country.

Perhaps even more important than projects such as these was the training that the Directorate organised at Tolworth and the assistance it gave to the British Council to place students at British colleges and universities. Courses at Tolworth were individually tailored to the needs of the overseas students and began in about 1958. From then until 1984, it is estimated that some 500 students studied carto- graphy, photogrammetry and photographic procedures. Training at the Directorate seemed to have much the same bonding effect as going to the same school or university. An enthusiastic Training Officer, Jock Reading, had blazer badges, ties and plaques made and these were eagerly bought by the students. The students' program- mes and their welfare was looked after by Irene Meux and Barbara McHugo successively, both of Technical Services. Their success can be judged by the fact that, when McHugo retired, nearly one hundred students wrote to wish her well. The Solomon Islands contingent provided an interesting list of the jobs they had ended up in:

Chief Administration Officer	Clerk to Guadalcanal Province
Principal Cartographer	Minister, Methodist Church
Senior Cartographer	College of Higher Education
Cartographer	Deputy Commissioner of Lands
Assistant Cartographer	Provincial Government Members (2)

They may have received a technical education but their visit clearly must have broadened their capabilities in many other ways too. As a Cypriot ex-student said in a letter at the same time:

> I shall never forget the kindness, politeness and real interest of all the staff of DOS shown to me. Still I remember [after 17 years] my instructors – how willing they were to advise me not only in subjects concerning my course but for every problem I came across. [2]

In 1975, the Directorate worked with the British Council and the North East London Polytechnic to design and mount a unique course for middle managers in Survey and Lands departments overseas. The first course was a considerable success and further courses were held in 1977, 1980 and then at two-year intervals until 1992 – an indication of their continuing popularity with local managers. This interest in management as well as technical training stemmed, perhaps, from the style that the Directorate had brought to a series of valuable Commonwealth Conferences which it had been responsible for running since the War.

The Conferences took place at four-year intervals and had begun in 1928 as Empire Survey Officers' Conferences. Such events were common amongst the scientific disciplines in Colonial times and the Directorate provided an ideal source for the secretariat services that were necessary. The target audience was always senior managers rather than working surveyors. Presentations were confined to principles rather than detail. The Conference Secretary enforced a strict discipline on speakers who were expected to provide a copy of the paper well in advance for pre-circulation and then to take no more than fifteen minutes to present the salient points to the audience. The aim was always to allow discussion to occupy as much of the session as possible and, as themes of interest developed over the ten days of the event, arguments would mature over several sessions. Wright was Secretary for four of the events and did much to develop its down-to-earth style:

> The conference [is] held in a big [tiered] lecture-hall holding about 200 people. It seems probable that authors of papers easily get too big for their boots and it is much better for them to look up to their audience rather than down. Also, because a crick in the neck is very tiring, the audience are less likely to go to sleep if they are looking down not up; but few authors of papers actually go to sleep while presenting them. Sitting on a sort of high altar flanked by masses of flowers and national flags gives speakers and chairmen altogether too great a feeling of their own importance. [3]

It is an indication of the Conference's continuing appeal that it continues to convene every four years at Cambridge, the latest in the series, which now serves mapping agencies throughout the world, having taken place in 1995.

The Directorate's attitudes to conferences and trainees were very similar. There was a concentration on what the audience or the trainee wanted, and a package to suit the need was devised and delivered. To the trainees, the techniques and the detail were important. Training concentrated on technology that could easily be adopted in the trainee's home department. By the 1970s, this was seen by some as a paternalistic approach which denied Third World countries the benefits of computerisation. The Directorate argued that what mattered was to enable the trainees, when back in their own departments, to give a reliable service. This meant avoiding undue reliance on any complex infrastructure which might break down through lack of adequate funds for maintenance. This was typical of the 'no frills' approach of the Directorate. Ostentation was never part of its style, whether at conferences, in the drawing office or in the bush.

Chapter 22

Photomaps and Town Plans

When Warren had arrived as a Deputy Director in October 1965, the Directorate was tentatively beginning to consider the modernising of its mapping procedures. Though electronic distance-measuring techniques had been enthusiastically embraced in the field with great success, a more cautious approach had been adopted on the mapping side. By force of circumstance, methods had been adopted after the War which were low-cost solutions and the staff had become very adept at using and refining these methods. The presence of an instrument mechanic meant that small refinements could be constructed quickly with plenty of interaction and consultation. The instrument mechanic, Sid Ruston, became an important member of the team and was rewarded for his contributions with a British Empire Medal, after twenty-seven years' service, in 1975.

Warren had come from the Survey of Kenya, a department that had invested more than the Directorate in modern photogrammetric plotting machines. In Kenya, the task had been large-scale mapping but he was convinced of the value of the same approach for the medium-scale mapping that the Directorate was producing. He secured funding from ODM and began a major programme of investment. Over the five years from 1967 to 1971, 22 major plotting machines were bought and the staff were retrained to plot from aerial photographs by machine rather than by hand.

The Directorate became a major installation for PG2 plotting machines, manufactured by Kern of Switzerland. These were installed in a large room and separated by partitions, giving the appearance of a series of rather sterile animal stalls and acquiring the name of the 'PG Zoo'. It did not always look like this, however. One of the stunning events of the year at Tolworth was the annual Christmas Decorations. All the innate artistic ability of the staff burst forth in a truly amazing transformation of the Staff Canteen and the drawing offices by using waste cardboard and paper. Working in the evenings to a theme that had been agreed after much debate, they would create a Japanese garden complete with pagoda, or Venice with its gondolas and bridges. One year, the PG Zoo became a Dickensian shopping street. Each stall was a different shop: the butcher, the baker, the candlestick maker and so on. Inside each shop were all the objects you would expect to see, made of paper or board. Surrounded by his artefacts, the PG2 operator continued his work.

Warren also made his presence felt in field surveying and computing. The old Slotted Template Assemblies had had their advantages in the days when maps were wanted in a hurry and any map was better than no map at all. However, the emphasis had now shifted to regular national mapping programmes and less reliable results from the old methods were no longer acceptable. The new method of Aerial Triangulation by Independent Models took advantage of the arrival of the electronic computer and used complex mathematical formulae to produce the positional information needed to plot from the photographs. These formulae were much more sensitive to any deficiencies in surveyors' ground control. In such cases, very large errors could occur in the results. Warren insisted that the cartographers must therefore be able to specify the amount of control needed and where it should be. The surveyors would then have to go out and provide it. If they got there before the photographic aircraft, they would mark the control stations with targets which would show up on the photography and remove any uncertainty about the identification.

All this was a radical change from the Hotine era when surveyors had a very free rein to modify what was asked for in the light of any difficulties that they encountered in the field. Warren's action led to improved morale amongst the cartographic managers and to a much greater degree of contact and co-operation between cartographers and surveyors. It also allowed the Directorate to respond to the increasing numbers of demands for town plans that were now coming in from independent countries. Such plans were required to accuracies of a foot or less and this could only be achieved by the methods that Warren had installed.

The 1970s saw the completion of national mapping programmes at medium scale in many countries. Uganda, Malawi and Sierra Leone were the largest complete programmes but there were many other significant achievements: the whole of Botswana except for the remoter parts of the Kalahari Desert, the northern two-thirds of Ghana, much of north-eastern Nigeria, Belize, the West Indian islands, the major islands of the Bahamas and Fiji, Hong Kong at large scale, the Solomon Islands, Tonga, the coastal half of Sarawak and the eastern half of Sabah.

The majority of these maps were conventional line maps but, in countries and islands where there was little relief, photomaps were introduced from 1969. These were perhaps the most elegant and attractive of all the maps produced by the Directorate. The basic underlying map was constructed as a mosaic of the actual aerial photography, adjusted to scale. Superimposed on this was cartographic enhancement of the main topographic features: roads, settlements and vegetation. A judicious use of colour and a careful blending of photography and cartography produced a most attractive result. The vegetation and many water features, such as reefs, could be seen in all their complexity as they actually appeared on the photography.

The photomap was a product of the skills of the photographer and the cartographer and was a refreshing reminder that such skills were still valuable in a computer age. Photographers at the Directorate were not photographers in the commonly understood sense. They did not trail round behind the Director taking photographs with a press camera at regular intervals. Their job did not get very much publicity but was crucial to the accuracy and appearance of every map that was produced. They operated large process cameras capable of handling copy up to three feet square. They turned positives into negatives and negatives into positives, enlarged and reduced production material to precise tolerances, and processed the numerous prints of aerial photography that were needed. Without them, the maps would never have reached the printing presses. Yet, as a small group working most of the time in dark rooms, they tended to be invisible. They did, however, have their own ways of making an impact:

> The evening before I got married, I was stripped to my underwear, tied to a metal chair, put into one of the deep sinks and soaked with the hot and cold hoses. My clothes were also soaked and then spread out, one to each radiator or notice-board down the long central corridor and I was left to work out an acceptable way of recovering them. I cycled home in dripping clothes but survived to attend the marriage ceremony next day![1]

When he returned from his honeymoon, the same individual found a huge stack of job cards awaiting his attention, implying that no one had covered for him in his absence. The superintendents in the Cartographic Divisions had co-operated in generating false demands to give him a shock on his return. These practical jokes helped to build the strong sense of team spirit and co-operation that permeated the whole organisation and was so essential to its success.

The photomap was a classic example of what close co-operation between photographers and cartographers could achieve. However, the original idea came from two cartographers, A G L Bryant and J E Simms and it was they who were each awarded £300 by the Civil Service Department, on the recommendation of the Committee for Awards to Inventors. Photomaps were produced of The Gambia, the Okavango Swamps in Botswana and many Pacific Islands in Kiribati, Tuvalu and Tonga. They were universally popular with users.

The increasing demand for large-scale maps of urban areas and in support of rural development projects reflected a changing need in independent countries. One effect of the changeover to independence was the sudden arrival, in the new nation, of delegations from countries that had had little access during the Colonial regime: the Soviet Union, the United States, Sweden – all were keen to increase their influence by offering aid. This surge in interest led to a surge in demand for mapping that would help in the selection of suitable sites and the planning of the chosen project. Several projects were concerned with the resettlement of urban squatter communities and this provided a particular need for mapping of major cities. In 1980, the Directorate won a contract from the World Bank to provide 1:1,000 mapping of Monrovia, capital of Liberia, the largest scale of urban mapping it ever produced. The switchover in scale can be judged by the fact that, in 1968–9, the Directorate produced 190 maps at 1:50,000 scale and 43 at 1:5,000 or larger; in 1981–2, it produced 86 at 1:50,000 and 175 at 1:5,000 or larger.

Variety was added to the cartographer's work by the demands made by the Land Resources Division during this period. Production peaked in the mid-1970s when well over 100 maps per annum were being produced. These maps covered a wide range of projects: forest inventories in the Bahamas and Belize, development in St Helena, soil surveys in the Solomon Islands and land use in Zambia.

The quality of the cartographic work was reflected in a run of awards from the British Cartographic Society. Between 1978 and 1983, the Directorate won three Design Awards and was 'highly commended' on three further occasions.

Chapter 23

On the Edge

Changing scenes and changing attitudes had a major effect on the surveyor's life in the final years of the Directorate's existence – from the late 1970s onwards. New projects in countries with no history of British colonialism brought surveyors into contact with new cultures and different attitudes. The level of security declined in many countries and surveyors were caught up in outbreaks of violence. There were changes too on a personal level. The ease and relative cheapness of air travel allowed many girlfriends to spend extended holidays in the bush and many surveyors preferred an expedition-style life whilst on safari, declining to employ a cook even where they were still available. In many countries, cooks willing to accept the rigours of the bush life simply did not exist and surveyors had no option but to make their own meals on return from a hard day in the bush. Whether because of this or for other reasons, there seemed to be an increase in the incidence of diseases such as hepatitis. Even more than in the past, surveyors seemed to be living on the edge – the risks were greater but the willingness to take them was perhaps greater, too.

In the new countries such as Liberia, it was always difficult to find local people willing to carry loads up a mountain:

> We were at the village at nine but the men were not so I spent a frustrating day reading, drinking tea and watching people watching us as they passed by. We moved camp to the village in the afternoon and, in the evening, after a bath in the local stream, I took twelve names but still need three more.
>
> We left at 8.30 next morning and it took an age to reach the base of the hill. We followed footpaths through rubber trees, maize and cassava at first but then had to clear out old footpaths overgrown by secondary jungle. It wasn't a hard walk by normal standards but the casual labour took their time and rested often. At the foot of the hill, there was some small palava with a drunken man wanting cigarettes and money off me

and then a discussion with the casuals who weren't keen to climb the mountain after all, expecting me to climb up and down every day instead. Having convinced them it was necessary for me to stay up there, they enquired whether I really needed all the items up there at once. Eventually, it was all settled and we set off up through primary jungle on a slippery path, reaching the summit after a two hour slog. Following a short rest, I cajoled and insisted on them making a clearing and by 3.30, the camp site had been cleared, the tents erected, stove lit and kettle on, the (very) casual labourers paid off and the four of us settled in. [1]

The weather was always difficult in Liberia but, even so, there were rewards for the summit dweller:

About midday, we were hit by a big storm and I thought my tent would blow down but it survived although everything including me got very wet. Once the storm passed it was very, very still with no sound – very, very eerie. The view was surreal. A blanket of very low cloud, with mountains like islands poking out of the sea; as the sun set, the low cloud grew patchy but you couldn't see the ground between the patches, just a black void. Then the patches turned to a thin mist and it was as if you were looking through a glass topped table onto a model of the forest below. As it grew dark, there was only the odd speck of man-made light to be seen while, in the distance, frequent flashes of lightning lit up faraway mountain ranges and storm clouds. [2]

Life in a Liberian town could be more traumatic:

While driving in convoy of 3 LandRovers in Gbarnga, one dropped a track rod from the steering and crashed into transformer on side of road. Police arrested driver and I fixed vehicle. On returning to Police Station, the same thing happened again. Fortunately I was going slowly and slid into an embankment. While trying to get bail for driver, 2 other DOS employees were arrested for failing to stand up when Liberian flag was lowered. Situation was becoming rather farcical. Could not get bail for driver as magistrate 'not here'. Persuaded drunk police chief to release other arrested men. Returned to Suakoko for night. Police came to arrest me at 9 pm, taken off to Police Station and charged with reckless driving. Was interrogated then we all visited scene of the crime. Apparently I was also charged with damaging an embankment, could hardly restrain my laughter. Further interrogation by drunk police chief who eventually let me and driver go. [3]

When entering a new area, surveyors would make much play of the fact that they had come on behalf of the central government to make maps for the benefit of the nation. In this way, they hoped to gain the co-operation of the local people. In Yemen, this did not work. The local people did not want the central government to interfere in their lives and unfortunately regarded mountain tops as both safe retreats and strategic outposts in times of conflict. Anyone who showed an interest in mountain summits was therefore treated with considerable suspicion:

> While observing angles on Jebel Subayh, three spaced shots passed in mid-air and, after a short gap, I saw a puff of smoke where a bullet hit a rock 15 feet away. No doubt wrongly, I continued observing. The men with me did not seem unduly excited although those not actively engaged in the work did go to the 'lee' side of some rocks close by. An hour later, a fifth shot hit the rock beside Abdul Khadir, the helio operator, and splinters of rock cut his back and fingers of his left hand. The wounds were superficial. We then all got behind the rocks, I rescued the instruments after a while and we went down the hill by a protected route to our vehicle. We have heard of no subsequent developments. [4]

In some areas of the country, organised guerrilla groups were operating and it was very difficult to understand exactly where they were. Stephen Sykes, an Army officer on secondment to the Directorate, had one very unpleasant experience:

> After the usual curry and the obligatory game of dominoes, I turned in. I read a book on Watergate, which sported the Stars and Stripes on its cover, before dropping off. The next thing I knew was the rattling of tins in the cooking shelter adjoining my tent. Before I could leap out of my sleeping bag to chase off the marauding scavenger dogs I thought to be responsible, a couple of figures burst through the tent flap and confronted me. Armed with Kalashnikovs, they gestured to me to stay in my sleeping bag and kept their weapons pointing at my chest and head. They then proceeded to search the tent from top to bottom, stripping and unpacking everything. The book drew a very adverse reaction, its cover implying my apparent American nationality. My hoard of cigars, maintained for just such an occasion (the entertaining of guests, albeit more friendly than these), was examined with interest and I hastened to offer a few in the hope of improving my situation.
>
>   Meanwhile, outside, my cooking equipment and food store were

being taken apart. Even my water filter was dismantled. My men were similarly searched and then we were all invited to step into our LandRover for a journey up the mountain. By daylight, the mountain tracks were difficult enough but by night and without lights they were seriously hazardous. The only consolation was that we could not see the sheer drops. From the moment of their arrival, we were not allowed lights of any description, not even a match, but we were able to spot the twenty or so men who were surrounding our camp as we drove out.

On arrival at our destination, we were marched off and told to squat below a wall to await our interrogation. Eventually, a somewhat distinguished-looking figure emerged and began to question us in a whisper. After a thorough interrogation my men had to swear that I was British not American. They were then asked if I was an Army officer, which they denied.

The questioner now identified himself as one of the leading guerrilla commanders and proceeded to lecture us. Ours was not an innocent mapping project but, as with all aid projects, a cover for more sinister activities. My men were doing a grave disservice to their country by working for the project. I was supplying information to the CIA. We were told to leave the area and never to return and we were given a list of other areas we should not work in. We were to leave at daybreak and would be kept under observation until we were gone. Having been returned to camp, we did just as he suggested![5]

Fortunately for all concerned, new technology became available which allowed surveyors to fix their position from satellites. This could be done from the roadside or any other convenient point and the hilltops could be left to play their ancient role as refuges from the government! In spite of all the encounters with armed men, the Yemen project was a very productive one and over 150,000 square miles of the country, the whole of the inhabited area, was eventually mapped, the last areas by the Ordnance Survey after the Directorate had closed.

Out in the Pacific, there was still the sea to contend with. Tonga, with its 170 islands scattered over more than 100,000 square miles of ocean, provided its own peculiar challenges to surveyors whose experiences of long sea journeys to hostile coasts in relatively small boats was all but non-existent. Though South Sea Islands are everyone's idea of an idyll, conditions were frequently difficult and often dangerous. Getting to many of these far-flung and uninhabited islands involved long journeys well outside the range of the limited assistance that was available in an emergency. Few of the remote islands had recognised, safe anchorages and making a landfall was a tricky operation. The landing party had to use a small dinghy to beach on a rocky shore or to negotiate a passage through the coral reef to the calm waters of a lagoon:

'Ata is a strange volcanic island sticking straight up out of the sea, surrounded by cliffs 400–1200 feet high. We were landed on the narrow beach at the foot of the cliffs and left there for a week while our boat steamed back to safety in Tongatapu, 80 miles away. There are no fresh water sources on any of the Tongan islands and so an adequate water supply had to be landed as well as all the necessary survey equipment. We clambered along the steep, boulder-strewn beach until we found an obscure route up through the cliffs to the top of the island. This was only possible because we had with us a young boy who had been shipwrecked on the island for nine months (while trying to run away to New Zealand!). He was living evidence that things could go wrong – the weather could turn too rough for us to be taken off, the water could run out, we could be swamped while trying to get off the beach. An unreliable HF radio set was our only contact with the Tongan capital but, in the event, all went well and we returned safely.

Toku Island was a different matter. Here an outer reef guarded a typical Pacific atoll and the sea boat had to wait outside the reef while the dinghy took the landing party ashore. This operation could take up to two hours during which conditions could change quite rapidly. As the reef was crossed, big breakers could be encountered unexpectedly. On this occasion, the dinghy was swamped and its occupants thrown out into the sea. The currents round these islands were often very strong and I later found my plane table washed up on the opposite side of the island. Fortunately, the occupants of the dinghy were all rescued though one of them reached the shore with nothing more than a pair of swimming trunks and a transistor radio, which he had resolutely clung onto throughout the incident! It was three days before we could be taken off the island. [6]

It is perhaps only in retrospect that one analyses the risks inherent in such ventures. Sensible precautions were always taken but, in such remote seas, there were no coastguards, lifeboats or RAF Nimrods to set out on search missions. The fine line between success and disaster was illustrated one day when an outboard-powered 14-foot boat came in from an 8-mile crossing of the open sea to the shelter of a coral-fringed lagoon. The engine was shut down and raised out of the water prior to landing. To everyone's astonishment, there was no propeller. In the clear, still water of the lagoon, however, it could be seen lying on the bottom. The securing pin had sheared and the propeller had stayed on the shaft only by reason of its own driving force. Had the engine been stopped or even throttled back to idle out at sea, then the propeller would never have been seen again.

It would be foolish to suggest that life in surveying parties was either one long dice with danger or that it always ended happily. Much of the work was routine and proceeded from month to month without incident. But, in spite of all the precautions that were taken, there were tragedies: a labourer drowned in a boat accident in the Caicos Islands, three employees lost in unexplained circumstances on Mount Mlanje in Malawi, a young surveyor tragically killed in a road accident in Zambia, a labourer killed by a falling tree in the Cameroons. But, undoubtedly, the most tragic loss of all occurred in Sabah. Strictly, it was outside the work of the Directorate but it happened to someone who had previously worked for the Directorate for many years and it provides a graphic illustration of how close disaster could be.

Bruce Sandilands had gone back on contract to Sabah after several years' service with the Directorate. He already knew Sabah from this period and was assigned to some work on the international boundary with Indonesia. This was in very remote country and he was dropped by helicopter into a clearing in the jungle. Returning to such a virgin spot after the work is over is much more difficult than returning to a roadhead where well-established hunters' paths will converge and funnel the traveller to his intended destination. Sandilands completed his work and was returning to the pickup point when he fell ill. After a day's rest, he sent his porters on ahead:

5th: Started walking from camp, men went ahead. I told them to wait every ½ mile, they did stop but not long enough for me to catch up. The men left me without leaving any food. I got 3 hrs from the 3rd camp at dusk having missed the way losing 2 hours.

6th: Passed camp 3 at noon. NO FOOD. Felt I could make the river which I did by 2.30 but still no food. Rain. Slept under tree.

7th: Feet in bad shape, moved much more slowly with a stick. Looked for food without much success, found grass. I have three sardines left after this evening. Feel quite well, just weak, relaxed but hoping there will be action on Monday. Slept under tree. Rain from 3 pm to 8 pm.

8th: After a long cold night had grass for breakfast. Feet about the same, went to river 9.30, dried out and had more grass and water, later ½ sardine. I feel quite well except I need food. If people work fast I still think I can survive but this may be the last day I can walk, water and shelter 12 yds apart. Can I make it? Grass 18 yds, 2 sardines going rotten. Rain at 1 am, grass for supper. [7]

For the next seven days, he lay by the river, increasingly encumbered by an infected foot. He was slowly getting weaker:

16th: Fair night, little rain, right foot now painful. Journey to grass 50 ft, 50 minutes, very hard work. Sun was pleasant but made one drowsy. Got back 2.30, very exhausted. Hope rescue party is trying as hard as me. I also hope the labourers are safe. Weakness and my feet are getting worse, 2 weeks tomorrow without food, rain all night, flooded out, got very wet.
17th: Rain till 12. Tried to dry out, went for grass, most was still under water, made effort to replace bed with sticks.
18th: Rain in morning. Pain increases. Maggots in both legs, got grass and water.
19th: Got rid of 100 maggots, so painful that was unable to collect enough grass and water. Much weaker.
20th: Rain and flood at night, everything wet through, was delighted to hear plane at 4 [pm].
21st: Everything too wet to write.
22nd: A better day, only got just over a PINT OF WATER AND HANDFUL OF GRASS, MAY BE LAST DAY TO WRITE. HOPE TO GET WATER TOMORROW. IF I AM DEAD WHEN YOU FIND THIS PERHAPS CHRISTMAS DAY COULD BE MY DEATH. GO THROUGH THIS AND DO WHAT'S NECESSARY. [8]

The labourers walked out but Sandilands' body was not recovered for another two months. From his watch, it was deduced that he had indeed probably died on Christmas Day. There was considerable controversy over what had happened and who was to blame. The police questioned the labourers but no action was taken. However, the tragedy was not complete. Six months later, the headman of the group took his own life.

Chapter 24

Families in the Field

The 1970s saw a trend towards greater normality for surveyors' families. As many as a third of surveyors were now on secondments to overseas governments where they were generally doing office-based training jobs and had an entitlement to be housed properly. The existing field parties had become more adept at acquiring accommodation through a variety of channels and a lot of the work was now taking place in towns. New projects included the requirement for housing as part of the agreement. In the bush, field parties still worked on the basis of three to six-week safaris with a return to town in between but, on town surveys, many worked a five-day week like officials of the local government.

The traditional safari still retained its special excitement though, by this time, the return was more likely to be to a suburban street than to a camp on the edge of town:

> For the residents of respectable neighbourhoods of African regional capitals, having a DOS headquarters next door must have been to say the least of it, a mixed blessing. The best part, probably, was that for three weeks of every month the place was empty while the surveyors were out mapping. Then within hours of each other on the 26th of the month, trucks and LandRovers would arrive from different quarters and the quiet suburban house, yesterday the lonely kingdom of a huddled watchman, was suddenly transformed into a logistics nerve centre.
>
> Stores of all sorts were offloaded, 44 gallon drums were piled up to be taken to the petrol station, jerry cans were lined up for cleaning. Metal trunks full of papers, wooden boxes full of tins, camp equipment and survey instruments were shipped in, piled in corners, counted and taken out again. Gangs of African labourers manhandled and headloaded building equipment of indescribable varieties. Treasured personal effects were carried by hand by cooks and 'bookers' from the vehicle cabs to the surveyors' suddenly refurnished front room where the camp desks had all been re-erected ready for End of Month Paperwork. And then, as

155

suddenly as they came, a week later they would equally abruptly be off again.

It cannot have been all that much fun for the civil servants and University lecturers who lived next door. For one thing the surveyors had none of the 'style' of the District Commissioner going on tour. Their shorts and shirts looked like cast-off tennis kit. Headgear and footwear was idiosyncratic to put it kindly and most of the rules seemed to be there to be broken. So long socks disappeared at sundown and the surveyors turned up for evening drinks in bare legs and flip flops when everyone else was in leather calf boots to keep off the sandflies. If you were unwise enough to invite the boys in for an evening meal, one would come in a long sleeve shirt and tie, another in a rugby shirt (a *real* rugby shirt) and a third in a khaki T-shirt.

They also had oddities of behaviour. They shared with Otter (the Water Rat's friend in the Wind in the Willows) the strange characteristic of disappearing inexplicably in mid-conversation and reappearing unabashed a few minutes later. Being unused to living in houses they would often just wander off to look at the sky in a particular direction, sniff the air or call unintelligibly to a watchman. [1]

Married surveyors were, of course, more conventional! Out on safari, however, unconventionality returned. Children were growing up and beginning to share the adventures of bush life; Peter Gibbs' son was three when he went off with his father:

When Judy, my wife, was in hospital expecting our second child, I took Simon on safari with me. I was camped on the Botswana side of the Shashi River, a dry, sand river some 300 yards wide that formed the boundary with Rhodesia. One day, I had to cross over to build a survey pillar in Rhodesia and I left Simon with my cook, Jack Mountain, to have a picnic under the trees by the river. It was a cloudless day and I was surprised when, as we were finishing work, the headman pointed up the valley to where sunlight was glinting on water. There was a flood on its way down river. We hurried back and just managed to cross back to the Botswana side as the first fingers of the flood reached the ford. When we got back to camp, we were met by long faces: Simon and Jack were on the Rhodesia side! I could see their shapes in the dark on the far bank but the noise of the flood prevented communication. I later learnt that they went off and found a village to shelter in for the night.

Next morning the river remained high. Anxious to get some food and clothing to Simon, I constructed a raft from an inner tube and a wooden box. Then, starting some way upstream and pushing the box in front of me, I swam safely across. Encouraged by my success, I put Simon in the box and swam back in the same manner, egged on by cheering from our camp. We reached the bank safely but it was not until the following day that Jack was able to cross in safety. [2]

Teenagers too had their moments to remember:

When Dad was transferred to Kenya, I went to Arusha School set in splendid grounds under the shadow of Mt Meru. Whilst all the other children turned up in posh cars, I arrived in well-worn LandRovers or lorries. I received a lot of remarks about it but it was the only way to get about for us. On safari with Dad, I used to get some funny looks going through any village. A blond young girl sitting on the back of the lorry with all the tents and equipment and the lads who worked for Dad. I hated sitting in the cab and, on every possible occasion, I was up on top of the lorry. It could get a bit hairy at times, like when we were going down the side of the Rift Valley on a very narrow track. It was only wide enough for one vehicle at a time and it was a tight squeeze to pass any vehicle coming the other way. But when we met a rhino, there was no question who had to give way – us! That was the closest I ever came to a rhino and I was terrified – though whether the rhino or the long drop off the edge of the track terrified me the more, I can't say! [3]

As children grew older, the time came for them to travel home to a boarding school education. These unaccompanied journeys, though efficiently organised by the airlines, were always worrying for parents, thinking about all the things that could go wrong. The children themselves adapted far more calmly to the situation:

The flight from London to Entebbe was the usual good service, plenty of food and people to look after you. It was when I tried to get the connecting flight to Mwanza in Tanzania that things started to go wrong. Mwanza airport was flooded and commercial flights were cancelled. One of the pilots off the London plane had the same problem as, strangely enough, he lived there too. He managed to hire a light aircraft complete with pilot and offered me a lift. I jumped at it without looking at the plane first – if I had, I might not have been so eager. Out onto the tarmac we went and there was this single-engined Cessna waiting to take me across Lake Victoria. What would Mum say? I was only fourteen, after all!

I climbed into the back and settled down for the flight. As we were going down the runway ready to launch into the blue sky, I looked back and saw this huge VC10 coming in to land. It was getting bigger by the second and I was sure we were doomed but at the last moment we lurched into the air and out of its path. I hoped that that was the last of any frights and tried to make myself comfortable. All of a sudden, it went awfully quiet, the engine had stopped and we were getting closer and closer to the water. All I could think was that I had missed being squashed by a VC10 only to drown in the Lake. At the last minute, the engine came to life again and up we went. The pilot told me that he was worried about the fuel level and was trying to economise. To say I was now very scared is to put in mildly! All I wanted was to get to Mwanza and never see a single-engined plane again. It was a big relief to everyone when we slithered to a stop in a cloud of spray. Mum and Dad were delighted to see me – but not half as much as I was to see them![4]

Families were now an accepted part of the overseas life. The old arrangements of serving double tours to make up for the extra passage costs had long since gone and bachelors and married men were on similar terms. Married surveyors received larger overseas allowances and could incur further cost to the Directorate for air passages for children at school in Britain to travel out twice a year. It was the bachelors' turn to feel aggrieved. They thought, perhaps perversely, that they lived a rougher life with no home comforts at the end of the month. They cost less to keep in the field but there was no acknowledgement of this. The wheel had truly turned full circle. This was perhaps accentuated by the lack of any changes to camp equipment in response to the rise in living standards during the 1970s. Every surveyor could still have his soda siphon but a fridge for use in the field was never a standard issue:

Most days in Yemen I climbed a hill. Half an hour was a short climb, most took 1-1½ hours, 3 was not unknown, all under a hot sun. I found the thirst these climbs induced particularly hard to endure. On one fly camp in Yemen I was miles up a wadi on my own. I had a tiny hot little tent in which to spend an uncomfortable night, it being better inside, hot and free from insects, than outside, cool and bitten. I was desperate for a cool drink but had to boil the water for health reasons. I needed to flavour it as I craved some sort of taste as well and, since I couldn't wait for it to cool, I drank pot after pot of hot fruit cordial and still couldn't kill the thirst. On my second tour in Kenya, I thought that I would be smarter and take a thermos filled with ice cold cordial from the kerosene fridges which the Kenyan party had acquired for a one-off job in the Southern Sudan. On the first day I took them out, I returned to the LandRover after a hard walk, only to discover the glass had broken during the rough trip. I was all but weeping with frustration as I tried unsuccessfully to strain the drink through my handkerchief.

Thirst and one's own company were bad enough in the bush but, even back in base, a bachelor could become very bored. Without a wife in base to build up contacts, it could take nine of the 12 months' tour to get to know anyone outside the survey party. A social life would then really develop during the last two months at which point it was time to move on! I certainly never felt that single surveyors got a very good deal. [5]

Whatever the rights and wrongs of this point of view, there were several resignations caused by similar feelings. It was perhaps inevitable that, with such an unusual job on offer, it would always be difficult to satisfy everybody. For those who felt the need for an occasional spell of duty at home, a useful development had been the creation of a Joint Survey Service in 1968. A selection of posts in the Ordnance Survey and the Military Survey Service were grouped with those in the Directorate, and a joint management committee from the three organisations arranged postings. This helped the development of broader careers for surveyors but, again, not everyone approved of the introduction of these home-based posts.

Like any organisation, the Directorate had its prejudices. It had long been the view that a surveyor's job could not be done by a woman and a raft of reasons had been advanced for this – too strenuous, the local male employees in Africa and Arabia would not take instructions from a woman, etc. etc. When the Equal Opportunities Act became law, the Directorate therefore applied for exemption from the requirement to offer surveyor jobs to both men and women without discrimination. However, it rapidly became obvious that, with the rest of the surveying profession opening its doors to women, the Directorate's position could not be sustained and, in 1980, the first female surveyor, Clare Hadley, was recruited. She found no difficulty in working in Liberia and Malawi. When Julia Hopwood joined the organisation after it had transferred to the Ordnance Survey, she found herself posted to Yemen. There had always been fears that this would be a particularly difficult assignment for a woman but, again, these fears were proved groundless:

Although Yemeni women eat and live, for the most part, separately from the men, their menfolk had little or no difficulty in accepting me as an 'honorary man'. Only once was I banished to the fire where the women were cooking – there, mustering all the Arabic I knew, I tried to engage in friendly conversation but I felt hostility from them as well. This was unusual and, on many occasions in the villages, women would stop me and ask me to take their daughters away so that they could do as I had done. I was certainly very well looked after, if sometimes a source of great amusement. Once a group of women insisted on feeling me up and down to convince themselves that I was indeed female.

In fact, the whole tour could have been a financial success for my employers had a Bedouin sheikh's attempt to buy me for the equivalent of £50,000 been successfully negotiated on their behalf. My Ethiopian driver might have had something to say about that, however – his intention was an even split between him and myself. However, he did not encourage me too much until I was offered a deal with one week's trial after which, if not satisfied, I could keep the money and return to Sana'a. He could not believe that I could turn that down![6]

The story was the same in all the countries in which female surveyors worked. They were welcomed and accepted. At the closing down party for the workforce in Malawi, Julia Hopwood was nominated by popular acclaim to fulfil the role of serving the *chibuku*, or local beer, a traditional woman's task in that country. Much had happened since, thirty-six years earlier, Walter Smith had argued with Hotine to have his wife out on a short visit.

Nevertheless, as the Directorate entered the 1980s, though the old enthusiasms still survived and though life for a surveyor was generally far more civilised, there was a downside. The field-survey operation had, for a range of reasons, become more expensive and, understandably, some of that sense of urgency of the early days had been lost. With a new Conservative Government in power, led by Margaret Thatcher, this issue of cost was to prove a source of considerable debate as Ministers searched for yet more ways of reducing the role of Government.

Chapter 25

End of an Era

Warren was due to retire as Director in July 1980. The new Conservative Government had announced its determination to reduce the number of civil servants and to transfer to the private sector work that, in its view, could be done there more effectively. To this end, the Prime Minister created an Efficiency Unit headed by Sir Derek Rayner, a senior executive from Marks and Spencer plc. Rayner introduced a programme of scrutinies, known as Rayner reviews, which he described in these terms:

   i)   The purpose of the scrutinies is action, not study. It is therefore:

        a) to examine a specific policy, activity or function with a view to savings or increased effectiveness and to question all aspects of the work normally taken for granted;

        b) to propose solutions to any problems identified; and

        c) to implement agreed solutions, or to begin their implementation, within 12 months of the start of the scrutiny.

   ii) This means that the purposes of the scrutiny reports are:

        a) to analyse what has been found; and

        b) to offer a basis (costed to the maximum possible) on which action can be taken. [1]

Edwin Furmston was to succeed Warren as Director. He had joined the Directorate as a surveyor in 1953 and was, at this time, Deputy Director (Field Surveys). His was the first and, as it turned out, the last appointment to the post of someone whose career had been spent almost entirely within the organisation. On the day that he received his letter of appointment at home, he arrived at the office to find that Warren had been told by ODA of yet another investigation:

I fear I have to impose yet another burden on you and your staff.
Ministers have decided that each year one aspect of the work of each

Government Department shall be subjected to a formal Scrutiny . . .

You might well ask why DOS has been selected for a Scrutiny especially as you are only now recovering from the turmoil inflicted on you as a consequence of a possible move to East Kilbride. While I would share your thoughts and emotions on this point, I have to tell you that the idea of making DOS the subject of a Scrutiny came from the Prime Minister herself.

In these circumstances, none of us here could see any point in raising objections to the proposal; they would not be well received and in the end they would change nothing. [2]

There was much speculation about the Prime Minister's involvement in the affairs of such a small element of the Government machine but no reasons were ever made public. Warren felt that the proposal came at a bad time:

Certainly with all that has been happening over the last few years and whilst we are still reeling from the effects of the dispersal issue, the freeze on recruitment and the latest cuts, it would not be possible to choose a worse time to look objectively at performance, costs, demands, morale and so on. [3]

It was decided that the Scrutiny would take place immediately after Warren's departure as he was worried that the staff might feel that a Director literally on the point of retirement might not represent their interests as forcefully as a new man. An Economics Adviser at ODA, G A Armstrong, was appointed as Scrutineer and commenced work in July 1980 with the following terms of reference:

To identify how DOS calculates the costs and benefits of the various services, principally mapping and revision mapping, that it provides to aid recipient countries either directly from its core budget or indirectly as part of other ODA projects.

To compare the costs of DOS services with the cost of similar services provided by private sector bodies and to identify the messages to be deduced from the results of this comparison.

To draw conclusions, and make recommendations for changes in the scope and type of services provided as may be necessary, including their cost and timing, and the possibility of making changes, on a selective basis, for them. [4]

The Review took four months. Armstrong found that a fair comparison of productivity and costs with those of the private sector was 'a particular problem' and recruited an independent Technical Assessor, Brigadier G A Hardy, to assist him. Hardy was a retired Army officer who had spent his career in Military Survey and the Ordnance Survey.

The principal conclusion of the Scrutiny was that the Directorate should be reduced in size by 65 per cent and relocated at Southampton as an Overseas Division of the Ordnance Survey within three years. The reduced unit would provide advisory, library and contract management services but the bulk of the map production activity would be contracted out to the private sector. This conclusion was supported by a report of over a hundred pages of complex and sometimes contradictory arguments. Its length contrasted with that of the Lane Report of 1971 which had reached similar conclusions in twenty-five pages.

Armstrong interviewed a wide spectrum of officials, academics and private sector companies. Many of his conclusions were strongly disputed by the Directorate management. He brought out into the open some of the tensions that had existed for many years between some officials at ODA and the management at the Directorate:

> . . . the reality for most of the programme is that projects are selected by DOS itself in consultation with local survey departments. ODA's project decision procedures do not operate so as to ensure that the work programme reflects genuine developmental needs and aid priorities because they have no effective link with the provision of finance for project execution . . .
>
> The volume of output from DOS is broadly determined by the volume of resources made available annually by ODA HQ independently of genuine demand criteria. What is produced, given these resources, is determined largely by DOS themselves on their own judgement of priority need.[5]

These criticisms were nothing new – they have been described in Chapter 14 at the time of the creation of the Department of Technical Co-operation in 1961. They implied, however, that all the controls introduced since then – five-year plans, the Advisory Committee, the Management Committee, clearly defined projects such as those in Ethiopia, Yemen and Sudan, supported by Embassies and geographical desks – had in some way been subverted by one Director exploiting the inflexibility of the Treasury Vote system.

Whether this was true or not, the Armstrong review reveals an inability within ODA to assign clear and workable responsibilities and then to observe them. To impose complex approval procedures on a Director who was responsible for the work of 400 employees was always going to risk misunderstanding. To ODA officials trained to apply common rules of project appraisal to the proposals that came before them, it was irritating to see survey and mapping projects avoiding the competitive process. This irritation was perhaps reinforced by the suspicions of collusion that were aroused by the unusually close contacts that existed between overseas Survey Departments and the Directorate after thirty-four years during which Directing staff had made regular visits and arranged extensive training for the upcoming staff of those departments. Few other Aid sectors, if any, enjoyed such close contacts.

Armstrong criticised the Directorate for adopting too high a standard of mapping for many of the territories in which it worked. This too was resented by the management which saw it as a slur on their professional competence and judgement. The argument reflected the rising power of economic short-term arguments in the 1980s. Mapping had to be justified by immediate need, not as a resource to be tapped as required over time. In truth, mapping can rarely be justified by a single short-term peacetime application unless it can be shown that a project would be impossible to carry out without it. But the surveyor can point to crises where the need for mapping has been so urgent and desperate that it could never have been produced in time from scratch. The Falkland Islands were mapped by the Directorate in 1959–60 and those maps were crucial to the success of the military expedition to recover the Islands in 1982. Large-scale mapping of the Lockerbie area in Scotland was vital during the widespread field-by-field search for remnants of the Pan American 747 in 1988 and was instantly available from the Ordnance Survey. There seems to be some difficulty in assessing the cost-benefit of these events for such an assessment has never been undertaken. Armstrong gave no credit for the servicing of such emergencies, confining himself to noting the need for evaluation.

Perhaps the most controversial of the Scrutiny's conclusions arose from its comparison of costs with the private sector. With many qualifications about the difficulty of comparing costs in field survey and map production, Armstrong nevertheless went on to suggest very significant differences between the Directorate and the private sector. Directorate costs were purported to be much higher though, because of the exceedingly complex nature of the calculations, Armstrong was unable to explain how differences of the size that he was suggesting arose. Furmston believed that much of the difference could be explained by unreliable data. Indeed, of the five cartographic jobs that were compared, the Directorate's costs varied from 30 per cent less to 60 per cent more than the private sector's. With such volatile data, the selection of genuinely comparable work was clearly critical to obtaining a fair result.

Nevertheless, Armstrong was impressed by the *esprit de corps* and the commitment that he found at the Directorate. He believed that his solution would preserve that *esprit* at Southampton and that ODA would continue to finance Aid mapping albeit at a lower level. In the Preface to his Report, he coated the bitter pill with these genuinely complimentary words:

> In considering the analysis and recommendations of this report it might be borne in mind, where there is criticism of the existing situation, with rare exception, it relates to the administrative framework within which the staff operate rather than the competence or application of the staff themselves. For 35 years the staff of DOS have, under very trying circumstances, made strenuous efforts to provide appropriate surveying and mapping services to the Third World. It has, and continues to be an effort of which, in my view, Britain can be very proud.[6]

Furmston was given three weeks to comment on the draft Report before he was told in December 1980 that the final text was going forward to the Minister. Staff representatives were allowed to comment during April 1981 but all this achieved was an assurance that the alternative option of a relocation to Military Survey at Feltham would be evaluated. In June, the Prime Minister endorsed the recommendations and, on 7 July 1981, Furmston was told of the outcome by Neil Martin, the Minister for Overseas Development. The Directorate would be run down in size by 65 per cent and it would move to Southampton in about 1984, at which time it would cease to exist as a special unit of ODA and would become a Division of the Ordnance Survey.

Many of the staff had, in the political climate of 1980, seen the end as inevitable. The Staff representatives had presented a statesmanlike submission which began with a quotation from John Ruskin:

There is hardly anything in the world that some man cannot make a little worse and sell a little cheaper, and the people who consider price only are this man's lawful prey. [7]

While unremittingly opposed to the break-up of the Directorate, they did 'reluctantly accept the underlying policy/political decision that Aid financed survey and mapping may be reduced'. [8] A reduction of 40 per cent was proposed in place of 65 per cent and the Military Survey unit at Feltham was suggested as a more satisfactory home than the Ordnance Survey at Southampton as it would avoid disruption for staff. Interestingly, the staff representatives had undertaken their own customer survey of consultancies, engineers etc. to establish the demand for maps. 38 out of 49 questionnaires were returned – an impressively high sample. 86 per cent said that mapping was essential for their work and 50 per cent required 1:50,000 – results that conflicted with some of the statements made by Armstrong in his Report.

In the months that followed, the Feltham option was evaluated and rejected in favour of the original proposal to move to the Ordnance Survey. Plans were then made for the move to Southampton. There was a brief resurgence of hope for the staff when, in the autumn of 1983, the House of Commons Foreign Affairs Committee looked at the ODA Special Units in some detail but the Government had little difficulty in disposing of their rather weak recommendations. The move of staff began on 2 April 1984 and, on 28 February 1985, when the last of them were ready to leave, Edwin Furmston, at a small ceremony, unscrewed the brass name plate, locked the door for the last time and handed the keys to the security men who were to defend the building from the vandals. Theirs was to be a long job – the site remained untouched and undeveloped until 1995.

Postscript

Too little time has perhaps elapsed to judge the outcome of either the closure or the consequential merger. Shridath Ramphal, Secretary-General of the Commonwealth, expressed his doubts when he opened the Conference of Commonwealth Surveyors in 1983:

> I know I speak for a great many in the Commonwealth and beyond in paying tribute to the Directorate of Overseas Surveys and its staff here and in any one of the many countries of the world in which it has provided a service. Since 1946 when it was safely delivered to its Bushy Park home by that remarkable organisational midwife, Martin Hotine, the DOS has in its own unobtrusive way developed a reputation for excellence which has been thoroughly well earned. [1]

After admiring the imperturbability with which the Directorate had adjusted to the many changes of guardianship that it had experienced in recent years, Ramphal went on:

> But the change which is about to take place is, I believe, more substantial and raises doubts about the security of its future capacity to serve an established constituency. I know that all its ardent supporters in Commonwealth countries will wish to see its particular identity preserved and its special ability to promote the cause of development maintained and indeed enlarged. This Conference by its expression of confidence in the role of DOS can, I am sure, help to secure the future of a very special service which may have emerged out of times past but remains relevant to the needs of the different times that have succeeded. [2]

What can be said is that *esprit de corps* does not travel, even to another organisation which is welcoming and which has its own equally strong and very similar traditions. It is a product of a particular environment and a particular set of circumstances. If either changes, it inevitably begins to wither. Nor have survey and mapping prospered under the internal evaluation process of Aid projects at ODA. Of the six private sector companies which helped Armstrong in his Review, only two remain in business. Most of the staff employed on overseas work at the Ordnance Survey after the merger have been deployed elsewhere. The Overseas Surveys Directorate has been retitled OS International and is finding a new role as a consulting organisation, with interests extending to Eastern Europe as well as its former constituency.

Many of the staff, reflecting on events, might now agree that closure was inevitable; that the Directorate had been born of a particular era and was no longer suited to the political imperatives of the day. All would, however, wish that the organisation and its employees had, after so many years of committed service to a high ideal, been spared the humiliation of being closed down on the grounds of a cost comparison that so few could believe was fair.

The Directorate was born of an idealism that was rooted in the responsibilities of Empire, and at a time when the ability of civil servants was rarely challenged. Its demise was the result of an arguably less idealistic allegiance to cutting the cost of Government, and at a time when private enterprise was held to be the paragon.

During its thirty-eight-year history, the Directorate mapped over 2,000,000 square miles of the Earth's surface – an area roughly twice the size of Western Europe – and remapped a quarter of that area to reflect its growing development. However inevitable its end, it is impossible not to regret the passing of the family feeling that brought 200 people to a reunion in 1994, nearly ten years after closure; of the enthusiasm that drove surveyors through blizzards in the high mountains of Lesotho and dust storms in the deserts of the Sudan; of the enthusiasm and professionalism that impressed so many visitors to Tolworth. Those who served in it, whether at home or abroad, can be rightly proud of the personal skills that provided so many fine maps to so many countries.

The Directorate played an honourable – and unconventional – part in the history of the British Civil Service.

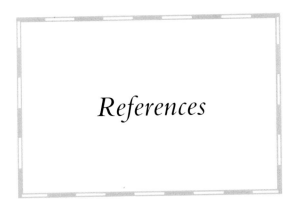

References

Introduction

[1] McGrath, G, 'Mapping for Development, the Contributions of the Directorate of Overseas Surveys', *Cartographica*, Vol. 20, Nos 1 and 2, 1983.

Chapter 1

[1] Seymour, W A (ed.), *A History of the Ordnance Survey*, Folkestone, Dawson, 1980, p 135.
[2] Ordnance Survey, Annual Report to 31st December 1858.
[3] Cd 1790, pp 36–41.
[4] Colonial Survey Committee, 'The Surveys and Explorations of British Africa', Annual Report of the Colonial Survey Committee (Cd 2684), HMSO, 1906.
[5] PRO OS 1/61 (OS File CR 7838), Item 31A, 1933. Copy in OS Library (Acc. no. 1924).
[6] MacLeod, Brigadier M N, DSO, MC, 'Imperial Geodetic Responsibilities', Paper to the Empire Survey Officers' Conference, Cambridge, 1935.
[7] Royal Society, *Report to the Economic Advisory Committee on Geodetic Work in the Empire*, April 1936.
[8] PRO OS 1/159 (OS File CR 11094/1), Item 12A.
[9] Ibid., Item 14A, 4 July 1939.
[10] Ibid., Item 22A.
[11] Ibid., Item 20A.
[12] Ibid., Item 23A.

Chapter 2

[1] PRO OS 1/159 (OS File CR 11094/1), Item 29A.
[2] Ibid., Item 50A.
[3] Ibid.
[4] Ibid., Item 60A, 12 May 1942.
[5] Ibid., Item 81B, 'Colonial Surveys'.
[6] Ibid., Item 74A, 4 September 1942.
[7] Ibid.

[8] Ibid., Item 87A.

[9] PRO OS 1/1160 (OS File CR DG 106), Item 34A, 6 October 1942.

[10] Ibid.

[11] Ibid., Item 39A, 21 October 1942.

[12] PRO OS 1/159 (OS File CR 11094/1), Item 101/1A, 2 March 1943.

[13] Ibid.

[14] PRO OS 1/160 (OS File CR 11094/2), Item 39A.

Chapter 3

[1] Hotine, Brigadier M, Letter to W P Smith, 24 July 1950 (in the latter's personal papers).

[2] Read, D, Personal Communication.

[3] Searle, Mrs P, Personal Communication.

[4] PRO OD 6/335 (DOS File 1002), Item 94.

[5] *News Bulletin*, Directorate of Colonial Surveys, 1 May 1948.

Chapter 4

[1] Brown, Mrs J, Personal Communication.

[2] Wiggins, W D C, Foreword, *DOS Gazette*, No. 22, 1967.

[3] Directorate of Colonial Surveys, Annual Report, 1946–7.

[4] Martkin, J H, Letter to H Green, 8 March 1960 (in the latter's personal papers).

[5] Wood, R, Personal Communication.

[6] Watson, W, Personal Memoir, 1980 (unpublished).

Chapter 5

[1] Watson, W, Personal Memoir, 1980 (unpublished).

[2] PRO OD 6/479 (DOS File 1053), Item 22.

[3] Ibid., Item 167A.

[4] PRO OD 6/478 (DOS File 1052/C/1), Item 15.

[5] PRO OD 6/477 (DOS File 1052), Item 62.

[6] *News Bulletin*, Directorate of Colonial Surveys, Christmas 1948.

[7] PRO OD 6/650 (DOS File 1002), Item 70.

[8] Bussey file, undated ms (at OS awaiting deposition in PRO).

[9] Hotine, Brigadier M, 'Surveying for Colonial Development' (discussion), *Empire Survey Review*, Vol. X, No. 77, July 1950.

Chapter 6

[1] Hotine, Brigadier M, 'Survey for Colonial Development', *Empire Survey Review*, Vol. X, No. 77, July 1950.

[2] PRO OD 6/125 (DOS File 502/3), Item 143, 7 April 1953.
[3] PRO OD 6/336 (DOS File 1002), Item 5.
[4] Ibid., Item 12.

Chapter 7

[1] Directorate of Colonial Surveys, Annual Report for the Year ending 31 March 1949.
[2] PRO OD 6/126 (DOS File 502/3), Item 56, 3 May 1954.
[3] Hotine, Brigadier M, 'Forty Years On', *Photogrammetric Record*, Vol. II, No. 8, October 1956, pp 114–5.
[4] Wiggins, W D C, 'Techniques used for the Mapping of Undeveloped Territories', *Nachrichten aus dem Karten- und Vermessungswesen*, Vol. V, No. 5, 1963.

Chapter 8

[1] Macdonald, A S, Personal Recollection.
[2] Green, H, Personal Communication.
[3] Macdonald, A S, Personal Recollection.
[4] PRO OD 6/509 (DOS File 1070/4), Item 38.
[5] Ibid., Item 122.
[6] Ibid., Item 128.
[7] Bere, C G T, letter to A S Macdonald, 22 January 1958 (in the latter's personal papers).
[8] Macdonald, A S, letter to C G T Bere, 1 February 1958 (in the former's personal papers).
[9] Green, P F, 'Eight Months up the Creek', personal memoir, (unpublished).
[10] Ibid.
[11] Gibbs, P M, Personal Communication.

Chapter 9

[1] PRO OD 6/467 (DOS File 1051/A), Item 22.
[2] Opie-Smith, P, Personal Communication.
[3] Opie-Smith, P, Personal Communication.
[4] Meggitt, G W, Monthly Diary entry, July 1957.
[5] Auld, J R, Personal Papers.
[6] Ibid.
[7] PRO OD 6/519 (DOS File 1070/5), Item 69, 29 May 1959.
[8] Cregeen, D J, Personal Communication.
[9] Wood, R, Personal Communication.

Chapter 10

[1] Hotine, Brigadier M, 'Survey for Colonial Development', *Empire Survey Review*, Vol. X, No. 77, July 1950.

[2] Alexander, J B, 'Trials of a Surveyor – Modern Version', *Empire Survey Review*, Vol. XII, No. 87, January 1953.

[3] Bardua, R A, Personal Communication.

[4] Meggitt, G W, Monthly Diary entry, February 1957.

[5] Kozlowski, P M, Annual Report, Kenya Survey Party, 1959–60 (held with other party reports at the Ordnance Survey, 1995).

Chapter 11

[1] PRO OD 6/480 (DOS File 1053/1), Item 1.

[2] Ibid., Item 2.

[3] Wood, R, Personal Communication.

[4] Opie-Smith, P, Personal Communication.

[5] Green, P F, 'Eight Months up the Creek', Personal Memoir, (unpublished).

[6] Bardua, R A, Monthly Diary entry, July 1958.

[7] Ibid., October 1958.

[8] Ibid.

[9] Furmston, B E, Monthly Diary entry, December 1957.

[10] Ibid.

[11] Newby, P R T, Personal Communication.

Chapter 12

[1] Empire Survey Officers' Conference, 1947, Proceedings, p 290, HMSO.

[2] Hotine, Brigadier M, letter to G J Humphries, 6 March 1950 (in W P Smith's personal papers).

[3] Alexander, J B, letter to Brigadier M Hotine, 1 March 1951 (ODA(DOS) File 52/36).

[4] Hotine, Brigadier M, letter to W P Smith (in the latter's personal papers).

[5] Ibid.

[6] Ibid.

Chapter 13

[1] Directorate of Colonial Surveys, Annual Report for the Year ending 31 March 1955, p 7.

[2] Directorate of Colonial Surveys, Annual Report for the Year ending 31 March 1959, p 10.

Chapter 14

[1] PRO OD 6/884 (DOS File 1600/1), Item 7, 1 October 1960.
[2] Ibid., Item 18, 12 December 1960.
[3] PRO OD 6/838 (DOS File 415/1), Item 3, 31 October 1960.
[4] Ibid., Item 5, 21 November 1960.
[5] PRO OD 6/884 (DOS File 1600/1), Item 35 (attachment).
[6] Ibid.
[7] Ibid., Item 35, 22 August 1962.
[8] Ibid.
[9] Ibid.

Chapter 15

[1] Directorate of Colonial Surveys, Annual Report for the Year ending 31 March 1948.
[2] Searle, Mrs P, Personal Communication.

Chapter 16

[1] Warner, P, Monthly Diary entry, November 1959.
[2] Macdonald, A S, Personal Recollection.
[3] Bloomfield W A, Monthly Diary entry, January 1958.
[4] Ibid.
[5] Bardua R A, Monthly Diary entry, November 1964.
[6] DOS File 56, February 1964 (since destroyed under statute).
[7] OS(DOS) File 1070/30, Item 49 (awaiting deposition in PRO).
[8] Ibid., Item 56.
[9] Rogers, H H M, Private letter to his parents, January 1964.

Chapter 17

[1] DOS File 56 (since destroyed under statute).
[2] Ibid.
[3] Ibid.
[4] OS(DOS) File 1070/30, Item 76, June 1966.
[5] Opie-Smith, P, Personal Communication.
[6] Allan, A L, Personal Communication.

Chapter 18

[1] Ayers, Mrs M, Personal Communication.

[2] Morris, Mrs J, Personal Communication.

[3] Weston, A, Personal Communication.

[4] Perla, Mrs A, Personal Communication.

[5] Ibid.

[6] Leonard, Mrs C, Personal Communication.

[7] Ibid.

[8] Anon.

Chapter 19

[1] Directorate of Colonial Surveys, Office Instructions No. 2, May 1946.

[2] DOS File 1400/48/1, letter from M Brunt to T A Jones, Trinidad, 20 February 1957 (since destroyed under statute).

[3] Lovell, C G, 'The Best Laid Schemes', Personal Memoir, 1984 (unpublished).

[4] Records General (Internal memorandum), possibly by J H Mankin, late 1951 (held at the Ordnance Survey).

[5] Warren, D E, partial transcript of retirement speech and B E Furmston's reply, 1980 (held in the Ordnance Survey Library).

Chapter 20

[1] Cmnd 2736, 'Overseas Development: the work of the new Ministry', para 32.

[2] Wiggins, W D C, Draft of statement to meeting at ODM, 18 October 1967 (contained in 'Value for Aid' file held at the Ordnance Survey).

[3] Handwritten copy in Hotine's hand (contained in a file of his miscellaneous papers held at the Ordnance Survey).

[4] Report of Working Party on the Directorate of Overseas Surveys, December 1968, para 54.

[5] Overseas Development Administration, Review of the Directorate of Overseas Surveys by Civil Service Department, May 1971.

[6] Cmnd XXXV–4814, 'A Framework for Government Research and Development'.

[7] Directorate of Overseas Surveys, Annual Report for the Year ended 31 March 1977, p 1.

[8] Cahill, M L, letter to D E Warren, 7 July 1977 (OS(DOS) File 274).

[9] Warren, D E, letter to Mrs K Hotine, 8 February 1979 (OS(DOS) File 274).

Chapter 21

[1] Norrie, A J, Monthly Diary entry, November 1976.
[2] McHugo, M B, Personal Papers.
[3] Wright, J W, 'Making Conferences Successful', *Nature*, Vol. 236, 17 March 1972, pp 101–2.

Chapter 22

[1] Page, G F, Personal Communication.

Chapter 23

[1] Cory, M J, Personal Diary, November 1981.
[2] Ibid., August 1981.
[3] Hartley, W S, Monthly Diary entry, July 1980.
[4] OS(DOS) File 224/216/06, Item 2.
[5] Ibid., Item 59.
[6] Bishop, G, Personal Communication.
[7] Sandilands, B W, Monthly Diary, December 1975 (held in OS(DOS) File 274).
[8] Ibid.

Chapter 24

[1] Aarons, J J, Personal Communication.
[2] Gibbs, P McC, Personal Communication.
[3] Court, Mrs J (née Morris), Personal Communication.
[4] Ibid.
[5] Kyle, Dr S, Personal Communication.
[6] Cogan, Mrs J (née Hopwood), Personal Communication.

Chapter 25

[1] OS(DOS) File 600/02, Item E1.
[2] Ibid., Item 1.
[3] Ibid., Item 2.
[4] Rayner Scrutiny Project Report, The Directorate of Overseas Surveys, December 1980, para 2.1.1 (Ordnance Survey Library Ref: 42967G).
[5] Ibid., Summary Report, paras 6 and 7.
[6] Ibid., Preface, para 2.
[7] OS(DOS) File 600/02, Item 39.
[8] Ibid.

Postscript

[1] Conference of Commonwealth Surveyors, 1983, Proceedings, p 5.
[2] Ibid.

Appendix 1

Chronology

1946	11 March	DCS opened at Block B, Camp Griffiss, Bushy Park, Teddington, Middlesex, with Brigadier Martin Hotine as Director, and five staff.
	May	First recorded cartographic work began: fair drawing of Jamaica 1:50,000 series.
	November	First Survey Party set up in Gold Coast under W P Smith (later Director General of Ordnance Survey).
1947	1 January	Post of Chief Cartographer filled by L D Carmichael ('Map Production Manager' from 1 August 1972).
	1 November	H H Brazier appointed Chief Computer in succession to C G Fannin (resigned 30 April).
	December	First 'Preliminary Plots' printed (in Tanganyika, sheets 97 and 117): usually monochrome and planimetric only, produced quickly to meet urgent needs, at scales 1:125,000–1:25,000.
1948	1 January	Post of Assistant Director (HQ), occupied by W D C Wiggins since opening of the Directorate, upgraded to Deputy Director.
	Sept–Dec	Measurement of Directorate's first primary triangulation base line, the Sambani Base, near Mulanje, Nyasaland.
1949	February	First large-scale urban mapping published – 1:5,000, Jesselton Area, North Borneo.
	August	Flying began under first commercial Air Photography Contract to be let by the Directorate (in British Guiana).

177

1951		Wallace & Tiernan altimeters introduced for establishing height control.
		Adjustment of the Arc of the 30th Meridian from Southern Rhodesia to Uganda completed ('New (1950) Arc Datum').
	18 June	Move of DCS from Bushy Park to Kingston Road, Tolworth, began.
1951/2		Several overseas students were given courses of instruction – the first recorded.
1952		First Print Laydowns (PLD) produced.
	September	82 Squadron, RAF, withdrawn from Africa; henceforth, great majority of mapping photography used by DCS was flown by commercial contractors.
	October	Surveyor W H Young sent to organise a cadastral re-survey of St Vincent, the first such work done by DCS.
1953	5 January	DCS announced that, from 1 July, new medium-scale mapping in East and Central Africa would be on New (1950) Arc Datum and Universal Transverse Mercator Grid (instead of East Africa Belt grid).
	2 February	First Land Utilisation Officer took up his appointment (until Dec 1954).
	22 October	HRH The Duke of Edinburgh visited DCS.
1954	January	Survey began of the Precise Traverse framework in Gambia.
	February	Soil Map of Central Trinidad, 1:50,000, printed in four sheets; the most ambitious multicolour job so far undertaken.
	Nov–Dec	Measurement of the Nachingwea Base, Tanganyika; a cine film of the field work was produced by Macqueen Film Organisation.
1955	3 June	First use of an electronic computer – Military Survey's Elliott 401 – for conversion of geo-

graphical to grid co-ordinates in British Somaliland.

1957	April	Measurement of the Isiolo Base, Kenya, the last traditionally taped primary base line, completed.
	1 June	DCS renamed Directorate of Overseas (Geodetic and Topographical) Surveys.
	June	First hill-shaded tourist map published – Mount Kenya 1:25,000.
	Aug–Sept	First use of electronic distance-measuring (EDM) equipment between Isiolo and Malindi, Kenya by DOS.
1958	October	H A Stamers Smith appointed Assistant Director (Air) in succession to Group Captain J Bussey (retired).
1958/9		Forestry and Land Use Section established, by amalgamation of Commonwealth Forest Air Survey Centre and Land Use Section.
1959		'Dual Scale' mapping at 1:10,000 and 1:25,000 from one set of scribed drawings, introduced for Cyprus (and, later, Trinidad and Tobago, Grenadines, Hong Kong, etc).
1960		Hill shading introduced on 1:50,000 first edition mapping, as interim step before contoured second editions (Sarawak, Nyasaland; later S Cameroons, Sierra Leone etc).
	19 February	First survey and mapping Mutual Technical Co-operation Scheme agreed with an independent member of the Commonwealth (Ghana).
	February	Electronic computing commenced on the Ferranti 'Pegasus' computer at Feltham.
	March	First programme of primary levelling begun in Uganda.
	June	DOS Catalogue of Maps published (previous, unillustrated, editions 1952, 1956).

	September	Super-Wide Angle air survey camera (120° field over view) used for first time, in British Guiana.
1961		Experimental Aerotriangulation by observation of Independent Models (AIM) computed on 'Pegasus' (for Bahamas).
	24 July	DOS became one of the specialist units of the newly formed Department of Technical Co-operation.
	December	New post of Assistant Director (Liaison and Cadastral) established ('AD (Survey)' from 13 August 1963); J W Wright appointed.
1962	October	Final version of the East African, 1:50,000 mapping specification prepared. Kuching sheet published as pilot sheet for new Far Eastern (Malaysia), 1:50,000 mapping specification.
1963	1 May	Mr C I M O'Brien Assistant Director (Air) in succession to H A Stamers Smith (retired).
	10 October	G J Humphries Director, in succession to Brigadier M Hotine (retired); J W Wright Deputy Director (Survey); C G T Bere Assistant Director (Survey).
	November	Following tests in 1962, first Kern PG2 photogrammetric plotter purchased; used especially with super-wide angle photography.
1964	February	First 1:1,000,000 sheet published on the 1962 International Map of the World specification (Tanzania: Lindi).
	April	Results issued for the last of the East African Primary triangulation and traverse network adjustments, designated as the 'New (1960) Arc Datum'.
	25 May	P C Chambers appointed Deputy Director of the expanding Forestry and Land Use Section (renamed the Land Resources Division [LRD] in July).

1965	August	'Expanded Home Base' scheme established by ODM, leading to considerable expansion in secondments of DOS surveyors and cartographers to overseas survey departments.
	1 October	W D C Wiggins Director, in succession to G J Humphries (retired). D E Warren appointed Deputy Director (Mapping).
1967		Major programme of photogrammetric re-equipment began, to increase aerotriangulation and large-scale mapping capacity.
	November	Electronics workshop established in Nairobi to service DOS and survey department EDM instruments; operated until May 1975.
1968	April	Regional Survey Officer system set up: RSOs appointed in Caribbean, Central Africa, West Africa.
	May	Joint Survey Service established, to provide for interchangeability of civilian professional survey staff between DOS, Ordnance Survey and the Survey Production Centre, Royal Engineers.
	31 May	D E Warren Director, in succession to W D C Wiggins (retired). Mr A G Dalgleish appointed Deputy Director (Mapping).
	December	Norwood Working Party recommendations included establishment of Overseas Surveys Advisory Committee in ODM, expansion into non-Commonwealth countries, linkage with a subject department in ODM, separation of LRD from DOS, deletion of words '(Geodetic and Topographical)' from DOS title.
1969	July	Colour cine film of the Directorate's work, 'Framework for the Future', completed; subsequently distributed to over sixty countries, and commentary translated into eleven languages.
	September	Regional Survey Officer post established in Malaysia (until March 1971).

	December	Following three years' investigations into the technique, two experimental photomaps covering Aldabra were published; many other areas followed.
1970	January	Transfer began of electronic computing from the 'Pegasus' to the new ICL 1902A computer at Feltham.
	August	First 'Dyeline Series' large-scale maps published: Betio (Gilbert Is), followed by Brikama (The Gambia) and many others.
	October	Caribbean Regional Cadastral Survey and Registration Project established; led and partly staffed by DOS personnel on secondment, and supported by DOS control densification, computing, survey equipment and large-scale mapping (Project concluded March 1980).
	4 December	Agreement signed for Joint Project in Ethiopia – the first major DOS survey and mapping project in a non-Commonwealth country.
1971	February	Civil Service Department review team (Chairman R K F Lane) began a study of the demand for DOS services and the best means of meeting it; expert assessor: W L Dickson.
	1 April	Land Resources Division of DOS became a separate scientific unit of ODA but continued to receive cartographic and other support from DOS on repayment.
	31 May	B E Furmston Assistant Director (Survey) in succession to C G T Bere (seconded as Chief Surveyor to Ordnance Survey, N Ireland).
1971		Deffa Offset Proving Press purchased: used for short runs of specialist maps and large-scale sheets which could not be printed by dyeline in the country concerned, as well as for proving tourist sheets and pilot sheets of new series.
1972	6 March	H H Brazier retired as Chief Computer, succeeded by Miss L M Windsor, 23 June.

11 May		The Lane 'Review of Functions of DOS' had recommended phasing out of DOS within 2–3 years; government now announced that staff would be reduced by 25 per cent and that mapping beyond DOS capacity would be contracted out to the private sector.
	September	Contract Control Section set up to arrange and monitor mapping contracts.
	November	First commercial mapping contract (No. 501) let – for drawing Kenya 1:50,000 Central block.
	December	Agreement signed with Lake Chad Basin Commission for aerial photography, survey and photo-mapping in all four countries bordering the Lake.
1972/3		British Antarctic Territory 1:250,000 mapping plotted on Multiplex from horizon-to-horizon tricamera photography.
1973	1 April	A B Whitelegg Map Production Manager, in succession to L D Carmichael (retired).
	July	W D Rushworth, Assistant Director (Survey) in succession to B E Furmston (posted to OS). 'Principal Survey Officer (UK)' post established.
	October	Regional Survey Officer post in West Africa closed down.
1973/4		DOS provided assistance to 61 countries, the maximum recorded in any one year. Multiplex phased out as a regular production method. Satellite imagery (LANDSAT) used for first time, to provide base maps for forestry mapping in Ethiopia and photo-maps of Antarctica.
1974	16 May	First meeting of new DOS Management Committee, replacing the Overseas Survey Advisory Committee.

	September	A P Atkinson, Deputy Director (Mapping) ('Deputy Director' after 1 September 1982) in succession to A G Dalgleish (posted to OS).
	November	Field work by Hunting Surveys began for Red Sea Hills 1:100,000 mapping block, Sudan – the only field survey contract let by DOS; work was supervised by a DOS project manager in the field.
1975		Work began on first major series of rectified mosaics, to be used for cadastral and development purposes (Guyana, 1:10,000, coastal area). ODM Review of the future of DOS took place under R H Belcher, following on from the Lane Review of 1972.
	October	First JMR-1 Doppler Satellite receiver purchased; used in Yemen Arab Republic to provide satellite datum (World Geodetic System 1972) values for the survey framework.
	November	Investigation began into production of a National Atlas of the Sudan, leading to a number of staff being seconded to the Atlas project in Khartoum.
1976	January	Full-time Regional Survey Officer post established for East Africa (since 1974 combined with duties of Project Co-Manager in Ethiopia).
	June	Field party set up for joint project to connect the Senegal–Gambia boundary to the Twelfth Parallel precise traverse, to provide a common datum for boundary surveys.
	July	The conclusions of the 1975 Review accepted by the Minister: DOS to continue for the foreseeable future though reduced in size.
	August	D W Proctor Assistant Director (Survey) (until February 1984), in succession to W D Rushworth (posted to Mapping & Charting Establishment).

	1977	Automated Drafting Equipment installed, mainly to produce base plots; associated PDP 11/35 computer also used for triangulation and photogrammetric adjustments.
	June	B E Furmston Deputy Director (Survey), in succession to J W Wright (retired).
	July	Memorandum of Understanding signed for Joint Survey and Mapping Project in Liberia.
	18 November	Decision announced that DOS should be relocated in Glasgow. Decision reversed July 1979.
	Nov–Dec	Experiments in four-colour printing, using the process colours magenta, cyan, yellow, led to publication in 1978 of the first three sheets (Dominica 1:25,000) using this method.
1978	10–11 May	Open Days held at DOS for senior members of the Diplomatic Corps, Government departments, universities, and professional bodies.
	May	DOS Management Committee agreed that DOS could accept map-revision tasks provided that they contributed to development.
1979		Two Santoni Stereosimplex G6 orthophotoscopes purchased; used in 1980 for experimental orthophotomaps of Cherangani Settlement Scheme, Kenya.
	June	B E Furmston Director, in succession to D E Warren (retired). A S Macdonald Deputy Director (Survey) until 1 September 1982. C J B Lane Map Production Manager, in succession to A B Whitelegg (retired).
	July	'Rayner Scrutiny' began.
	December	Miss L M Windsor retired as Principal Computer; succeeded by R S Waters and then by J E Farrow in January 1982.
1981	July	Regional Survey Officer post in Central Africa closed down.

	8 July	Recommendations of Rayner Scrutiny, that separate existence of DOS be brought to an end and much work passed to the private sector, accepted. ODA Steering Group set up to consider implementation.
1981/2		Training was provided for 41 overseas students, the highest annual total recorded at DOS.
1982	April–June	Emergency mapping of Falkland Islands, and supply of data and information, to support British Forces after the Argentinian invasion of the Falkland Islands and South Georgia.
	16 November	Prime Minister announced that, following the Rayner Scrutiny, the functions and complement of the reduced Directorate would be transferred to the Ordnance Survey.
1982/3		Survey Parties in Tanzania and Liberia contributed to the African Doppler Survey project.
1983	September	T D Shiell Principal Computer, in succession to J E Farrow (posted to OS).
1984	February	I T Logan Deputy Director, in succession to A P Atkinson (posted to OS).
	2 April	Overseas Surveys Directorate of the Ordnance Survey formed.
	September	Movement of staff and equipment to Southampton (began February) completed.
1985	28 February	DOS building finally closed; some map production, by staff not transferring to OS, had continued at Tolworth until end of 1984.

Appendix 2

Gazetteer of Aid

Post-independence names are given here. A further list, showing the pre-independence names, is at Appendix 4.

Key to Assistance

Air Photography	**A**	Land Resources Mapping	**L**
Survey	**S**	Secondments	**C**
Topographical Mapping	**M**	Training	**T**
Geological Mapping	**G**		

Country	Assistance	Country	Assistance
Anguilla	A, S, M	Chad	A, S, M, T
Antigua & Barbuda	A, S, M, C	Chile	T
Ascension Island	M	Christmas Island	L
Bahamas	A, S, M, L, T	Colombia	M
		Cyprus	A, M, T
Bangladesh	A	Dominica	A, S, M, L, T
Barbados	A, S, M, T		
Belize	A, S, M, L, C, T	Ecuador	C
		Egypt	T
Bermuda	A, S, M, T	Ethiopia	A, S, M, C, T
Bolivia	G		
Botswana	A, S, M, L, C, T	Falkland Islands	A, S, M, L
		Fiji	A, M, L, T
Brazil	T	The Gambia	A, S, M, L, T
British Antarctic Terr.	A, M		
British Virgin Islands	A, S, M, C, T	Ghana	A, S, M, T
		Gibraltar	A, S
Brunei	S, M, T	Gough Island	G
Burma	G, T	Grenada	A, S, M
Cameroon	A, S, M, T	Guinea	L
Cayman Islands	A, S, M, L, C, T	Guyana	A, S, M, T
		Haiti	L

Country	Assistance	Country	Assistance
Honduras	A	St Helena	A, S, M, C, T
Hong Kong	M, C, T		
India	T	St Lucia	A, S, M, T
Indonesia	A, C, T	St Vincent	A, S, M, T
Iran	C, T	Senegal	S, T
Iraq	T	Seychelles	A, S, M, L, C, T
Jamaica	A, S, M, C, T		
		Sierra Leone	A, S, M, T
Jordan	T	Solomon Islands	A, S, M, L, C, T
Kenya	A, S, M, L, C, T		
		Somalia	S, M, T
Kiribati	S, M, L, T	South Georgia and South	
Laos	G	Sandwich Islands	M
Lesotho	A, S, M, L, C, T	Sri Lanka	L, T
		Sudan	A, S, M, L, C, T
Liberia	A, S, M, T		
Libya	T	Swaziland	A, S, M, C, T
Madagascar	T		
Malawi	A, S, M, L, C, T	Tanzania	A, S, M, L, C, T
Malaysia	A, S, M, L, C, T	Thailand	G
		Tonga	A, S, M, T
Maldives	M	Trinidad & Tobago	A, S, M, T
Mali	T	Tristan da Cunha	M
Malta	A, S, M, T	Turkey	T
Mauritius	A, S, M, C, T	Turks & Caicos Islands	A, S, M, C, T
Montserrat	A, S, M, C	Tuvalu	A, S, M, T
Nepal	M, T	Uganda	A, S, M, C, T
New Zealand	T		
Niger	A, S, M	United Arab Emirates	G
Nigeria	A, S, M, L, C, T	Vanuatu	S, M, L, C, T
Oman	G	Vietnam	T
Pakistan	G, T	Yemen	A, S, M, L, C, T
Paraguay	M		
Peru	G	Zaire	T
Philippines	T	Zambia	A, S, M, L, C, T
St Kitts and Nevis	A, S, M, C, T		

Appendix 3
Prizes and Awards Gained by DOS

1947   Brigadier M Hotine (Director) awarded the Royal Geographical Society's **Founder's Medal.**

1952   W D C Wiggins (Deputy Director) awarded the Royal Geographical Society's **Murchison Grant** for contributions to cartography.

1955   Brigadier M Hotine (Director) awarded the Photogrammetric Society's first **President's Medal**.

1960   G F Reid (Surveyor) awarded the Royal Geographical Society's **Cuthbert Peek Grant** for contributions to Antarctic Surveying.

1961   J A Eden (Research Officer) awarded the Photogrammetric Society's **President's Medal.**

1964   Brigadier M Hotine (lately Director) awarded the Institution of Royal Engineers' **Gold Medal.**

1967   P Opie-Smith (Senior Surveyor) given the Royal Geographical Society's **Mrs Patrick Ness Award** for geodetic survey in the Solomon Islands.

1974   DOS 1:125,000 Tourist Map of Mount Kenya won for the Ordnance Survey the Supreme National Award, the **Thremmmy Trophy,** in the 3M Excellence in Lithography competition.

1977   D Read and C J B Lane awarded the Photogrammetric Society's **President's Prize.**

1978   Tourist Map of Aberdares and Lake Nakuru National Parks, 1:150,000, 1977, **Highly Commended** in the British Cartographic Society Award for Design in Cartography competition.

1978   A G L Bryant and J E Simms given **Civil Service Department awards** on the recommendation of the Committee on Awards to Inventors, for their work in developing the photo-mapping process.

1979   M H Mayes (Senior Surveyor) Joint Winner of the Field Survey Association's **Civilian Prize** for his work as survey consultant to the Krueng Jreue and Krueng Baro Irrigation Project, Indonesia.

1979   Pilot sheet for the new 4-colour specification Mauritius 1:25,000 series, DOS 329, Sheet 1, won the British Cartographic Society's **Award for Design in Cartography.**

1980   D E Warren (lately Director) awarded the Royal Geographical Society's **Patron's Medal** for contributions to survey and mapping, particularly of developing countries.

1982   British Antarctic Territory (north of 82°S) with South Georgia and South Sandwich Islands, 1:3,000,000, BAS (Misc)2, edn 1, 1981, won the British Cartographic Society's **Award for Design in Cartography.**

1983   Zanzibar 1:10,000 Sheet 10/2016, Zanzibar Town, edn 1, 1982, won the British Cartographic Society's **Award for Design in Cartography**.

1983   Geological Map of Swaziland, 1:250,000, DOS 1230, 1982, **Highly Commended** in the British Cartographic Society's John Bartholomew Award for excellence in the field of small-scale thematic cartography.

Appendix 4

Country Names

This table includes, exclusively, those countries mentioned in the text which changed name upon independence or for other reasons. Pre- and post-independence names are given. Countries which changed name without becoming independent are indicated with an asterisk.

Former Name	Present Name	Date of Independence
Basutoland	Lesotho	1966
Bechuanaland	Botswana	1966
Belgian Congo	Zaire[1]	1960
British Guiana	Guyana	1966
British Honduras★	Belize	1981[2]
British North Borneo	Sabah, Malaysia	1963
British Somaliland	Somalia	1960
British Solomon Islands Protectorate	Solomon Islands	1975
Ellice Islands	Tuvalu	1975
Falkland Islands Dependencies★	British Antarctic Territory[3]	–
The Gambia	Gambia	1965
Gilbert Islands	Kiribati	1979
Gold Coast	Ghana	1957
Malaya	Malaysia	1963
New Hebrides	Vanuatu	1980
Northern Rhodesia	Zambia	1964
Nyasaland	Malawi	1964
Ruanda-Urundi	Rwanda and Burundi[4]	1962

Sarawak	Sarawak, Malaysia	1963
Southern Cameroons	Cameroun	1961
Southern Rhodesia	Zimbabwe	1980
Sri Lanka	Ceylon	1972
Tanganyika	Tanzania[5]	1963
Zanzibar	Tanzania[5]	1963

[1] The original name from independence in 1960 until 1971 was Congo Kinshasa.
[2] British Honduras changed its name to Belize in 1973 and became independent in 1981.
[3] South Georgia and the South Sandwich Islands remain as a separate administrative unit.
[4] Two separate countries
[5] Tanganyika and Zanzibar were separate countries for some months before uniting to form Tanzania in October 1964.

Index

accidents and injuries 65, 76–7, 106–7, 119, 150 *see also* deaths

accommodation
  overseas 62, 118, 123, 155–6
  at Tolworth 83–4

Accra 73

Addis Ababa 139–40

Advisory Committee, Overseas Surveys 133–5, 181, 183

aerial photography *see* air photography

Aerial Survey of Forests, Committee on the 84

Aerial Triangulation by Independent Models 145

aero-triangulation 99, 180, 181

Afram River 37

Africa *see* Central Africa; East Africa; East and Central Africa; West Africa

African Doppler Survey Project 186

African Mapping, Department of 7

African Rift Valley 54

Agriculture and Fisheries, Ministry of 14

Aid schemes 93, 131–4
  allocations and funds 94, 95, 134, 135, 147
  British Aid Programme 133–4, 138
  conditions 89–90
  overseas 131, 133–4, 137
  for survey and mapping 165, 166

Air Ministry 40

air photography *see also* photography
  Britain and 30–1

in the Colonies 30–2, 44, 86
interpretation 49, 102
for land use information 49, 84–5
and mapping 2, 25
by private sector 98
by RAF 37, 39–41
and stereo-views 99
technology, new 99, 144, 146

Air Photography Contract 177

Air Survey Centre, Commonwealth Forest 179

Air Survey Unit 14, 18

air travel 76, 157–8

Aldabra 182

Alexander, John 80

Allan, A L
  on approaching Anguilla 116–17

Aloo, local labourer 69

altimeters 103, 104, 178

altimetry 103, 105

American Military Police 27

Anguilla 116–17

animals
  domesticated 76–7, 115, 121
  wild 38–9, 55, 62–70, 103–5, 118–19, 157

Annual Reports, Directorate 8, 34, 46–7, 50, 138

Antarctica *see* British Antarctic Territory

Appropriations-in-Aid 92

Arc Datum, New (1950) 178, 180

Arc of the 30th Meridian 178

Argentina 127

Armstrong, G A 166
  as Scrutineer 162–5, 168

Army
  Polish Army 26–7
  as surveyors 25–6, 85

Printed in the United Kingdom for HMSO
Dd 297432 C20 2/96

Challenger 'Mary'
Cape Point
(Cape St Mary)
10
Hotel

BAKAU

Dept of
Agriculture

FBM Bakau
50.61
Hotel
Fire
Sta
Bank
Market

FAJARA

Police
Depot
Public
Works
Dept
04
Katchikally
Sacred Pond

Medical
Research
Council

Hotel

BAKAU
NDING
(UC)

Government
Quarters

10
CS 205

Cape Creek

Independence
National Stadium

15.43
13/7

15
125 (SAT)

1/2
32.28

BAKAU
KUNKU

Hotel Staff
Training
School

Prison Camp

Camaloo
Corner

Kotu Stream (Kotu Sandu)

Old
Jeswang

Kaniting
Industrial
Estate

Cemetery

Kotu
Power Station
(UC)

Ampaya
Quarry
Public
Works Dept

Quarry

LATRI
KUNDA

Quarry

CT 3
48

Quarry

Police Barracks

O Y

Court

KANIFING
07

Clinic

njai
nda

Quarries

DIPPA KUNDA

Market

JESWANG

SERE
KUNDA

SARA JOB KUNDA

35.94
1/4

IBO TOWN

SABIGENDING

Bakoti

BUNUNKA
KUNDA

TALINDING
KUNJANG

20

Water Pipeline

(UC)

Faji
Kunda

36
KSM 61

LATRI SABIJI

Bajong
Kotor

Tabo Kotor

MFC

68
SD 1020

Abuko

Quarry
Sareh
Mowndeh

WELINGARA

017
124/GA78

15

CS 17.1
17

Waterworks

Sinki

ABUKO
NATURE
RESERVE

LAN

Kunkujang

Ker Dobaly